Praise for *Mother Me*:

Zara has presented information never before discussed,
information which is important to all adoptees and their children.
Having experienced separation trauma while an infant affects
the way a woman will mother her own children. Will they be able
to bond with their baby; will they be over protective . . . always
fearing someone will take him away?

Zara has incorporated experiences from various adoptees into
her text which give examples of how much motherhood has
affected them and how it has affected their children. This is a
much needed look at a subject that has been ignored by most
writers. I recommend it to everyone connected with adoption,
especially to female adoptees who are mothers or are
templating motherhood.'
Nancy Verrier, psychotherapist and author of *The Primal Wound*

an adoptee and mother of three myself, Zara H Phillips and
book *Mother Me* has touched parts that no other could even
know existed. In this sometimes overwhelmingly open and candid
telling of her story, she courageously digs deep, revealing and
confessing to the very real and raw emotions experienced by an
adoptee on her journey towards her self. Although at times I
found it painful to read, this is a powerful, heartfelt account
that is ultimately enlightening and uplifting. An essential read
for adoptees, regardless of gender, and important too for anyone
involved in the adoption circle.'
Nimmy March, actress, adoptee and mother

'This is a brave and compelling book. It's also a probably much
needed "how to" and "why to" step-by-step guide through the
awful emotional turbulence of adoption. Zara was always talented
and driven. Now I know why.'
Bob G

'As an adoptee who recently gave birth, I have been struck by how much adoption has re-entered my psyche. Phillips explores this issue in *Mother Me* with a rare and profound insight and contextualises it around her own fascinating story. It's an important topic and high time that somebody explored it.'
Kate Hilpern, journalist, adopted person and mother

'Many adoptive parents feel if they just love their adopted baby enough it will heal all their wounds. Parents need to be aware of the full range of issues they will face in raising an adopted child so they can recognise and deal with the inherent feelings of rejection and abandonment that occur when a child is raised by someone other than their biological parents. *Mother Me* is an honest portrayal of these and other issues.'
Paul M Fleiss, paediatrician, biological and adoptive parent

'Many adopting parents have no tools to understand the children they are adopting. This book is a voice from the inside. Its value and impact are more universal than we can imagine.'
Eliza Roberts, actress, producer and mother of Keaton and Morgan

Mother Me

An adopted woman's journey to motherhood

Zara H Phillips

Published by
British Association for Adoption & Fostering
(BAAF)
Saffron House
6–10 Kirby Street
London EC1N 8TS
www.baaf.org.uk

Charity registration 275689
© Zara H Phillips 2008

British Library Cataloguing in Publication Data
A catalogue record for this book is available from
the British Library

ISBN 978 1 905664 36 8

Project management by Miranda Davies, BAAF
Cover photo by Alex Madjitey
Inside photo by Jonathan Phillips
Designed by Andrew Haig & Associates
Typeset by Fravashi Aga
Printed by Athenaeum Press Ltd.
Trade distribution by Turnaround Publisher Services,
Unit 3, Olympia Trading Estate, Coburg Road,
London N22 6TZ

BAAF is the leading UK-wide membership organisation for all
those concerned with adoption, fostering and child care issues.

The paper used for the text pages of this book is FSC certified.
FSC (The Forest Stewardship Council) is an international
network to promote responsible management of the world's
forests.

Printed on chlorine-free paper.

FSC

Mixed Sources

Product group from well-managed
forests and other controlled sources

Cert no. SGS-COC-2482
www.fsc.org
© 1996 Forest Stewardship Council

Northamptonshire Libraries & Information Service

Askews

*To Zachary, Kayla
and Arden*

Acknowledgements

To Shaila, Miranda, Jackie, Michelle and everyone at BAAF, thank you for everything. Thanks also to Marlou Russell, Nancy Verrier, CUB (Concerned United Birthparents), Morristown Adoption Support Group, Liz Ashton and everyone at Barnet Adoption Team, and all the many people who have supported me along the way: Serena Roe, Anita Nurse, Katie Lachter, Roberta Rose, Lynne Oyama, Marion Mayer, Jeanette Ryan, Candace Calloway, Anna Ickowitz, Shirley Sharpe, Virginia Wiessmuller, Sandy Kugelman, Julie Dresel, Penny Anderson, Jimmy McCaffrey, Terry Dove, Melanie Redmond, Pete Briquette, Bob Geldof, Darryl McDaniels (DMC), Ronnie Paris and Pamela Slaton.

Thanks to my mother, father and brother, to Patricia, Roberta and Orlando, and to my birth father, Vittorio, wherever he may be. And finally, a huge thank you to my husband, Jonathan. Words are not enough.

About the author

Zara H Phillips is a singer/songwriter who spent much of the 1980s touring as a backing vocalist with popular singers and bands such as Bob Geldof, Matt Bianco, Nick Kamen and Perfect Day (supporting Bananarama). She is also a public speaker, leading workshops based on her experience of adoption, reunion, relationships and motherhood. Zara is married with three children and lives in New York, USA.

Note

This book is an updated, fully revised UK edition of *Chasing Away the Shadows* by Zara Phillips, Gateway Press, 2003, USA

Contents

Introduction

Writing this book has been a fascinating journey. As a whole, the experience has been truly cathartic. For a long time I wrote just for catharsis, not thinking much about who would read it, because if I did, I would want to start editing for fear of opening myself up to criticism and – even worse – hurting my family.

Initially, I planned to focus on how adoption had affected my experience of motherhood. When someone suggested that I include more of my life story to illuminate the developmental issues surrounding adoption, I found myself going back and forth. I debated what to add, what I should say, and worried over how the people close to me would react. In retrospect, wanting to protect everyone was actually a very adopted person-like thing to do. As a child I tried to protect my loved ones out of fear of abandonment. I am continually amazed that, at the age of 42, that instinct is still an integral part of who I am.

This is the second time I am completing this book. The first time was four years ago when I wrote about my experience for the adoption community in the US. I received some interesting feedback, with many letters not only from adopted people but also all members of the triad, telling me how much they identified with what I had said. This gave me the confidence to keep talking about this subject as truthfully as I could at the many adoption conferences at which I now present workshops. I never find this easy but I know that holding back would be a disservice to the work I am so committed to doing.

I realise as I revisit this book that things do change, feelings don't remain as powerful and hearts soften. I feel as strongly about the topic of adoption as I always did, but this time I hope I have more compassion for all sides of the triad. I feel a sense of duty towards those struggling to comprehend the impact adoption can have on a family and I feel deeply for the children who hurt as much as I did as a child, particularly when their feelings are not understood or validated.

Society needs to recognise children who have been adopted, or have been in and out of foster care, and acknowledge that they may experience grief and problems and sadness. What concerns me most are the children like myself, adopted as babies into middle-class homes, given all the trimmings, yet who grow up hurting inside, going through so much trauma where no one acknowledges their grief.

I just want people to think about adoption, not in the usual way – 'adoption is a wonderful thing, it gives the child a home' or, 'babies don't know if they are adopted immediately' – but to acknowledge that with adoption always comes loss. My hope is that society will truly recognise this loss and allow the children to grieve and allow the adoptive parent and birth parent to face their losses too. Adoption is a second choice for everyone.

This book is merely my own experience, a view of my life as an adopted woman. It is not intended to tell the story of any other individual. I am not an expert on adoption nor do I pretend to know all the scientific background, medical facts or statistics. I can only share my story, my feelings, for they are all I have. Not everyone who is adopted will have shared my experience – we are all different. Nevertheless, many of the issues I have had to confront and resolve will resonate with other people who have been adopted.

For me, adoption is gazing in the mirror and having no idea whom you look like. It is staring and staring at your adoptive family, searching for a resemblance and finding none. It is looking as hard as you can at everyone you meet and grasping at anything that could give you a sense of connection, the same colour hair perhaps or similar eyes, and feeling your heart skip a beat when you think that maybe you really do look like the man on TV, only to find out that he is a chief of police somewhere in Bosnia and you know that your birth mother never travelled. It is staring at families when you are at a party or meeting your school friends' mothers for the first time and being absolutely floored at how much they look alike, and as you babble on about their astounding resemblance, they look at you as if you have gone quite mad.

Adoption is growing up with a gaping hole inside that you want so desperately to fill, but you have nothing to put into it, no conscious memory of your mother, no idea of how you came into the world. All you have is your imagination to fill the void in any way it can: were you the product of a passionate love gone wrong? Rape? Incest? Indifference? Your inner world is populated with shadows in a murky background, shadows that never emerge into the light.

Adoption is living a lie, telling your family you don't care who your biological parents were so as to protect their feelings, while all the time your eyes patrol the streets, just in case "she" happens to walk by. Adoption is sadness so chronic you don't realise there's another way to feel, guilt for feeling that way and confusion about why you were given up.

In adulthood, adoption is perhaps a search, one that

takes years to complete or that never can be realised. Even with success, you may find that terrible hole is not filled by your birth mother, that she does not connect with you or show interest in the way you need it.

Nevertheless, I present this work in a spirit of great hope.

First, I hope that my book can be read by all people who have adopted children or are considering adoption. Adopting families and those contemplating adoption need to understand that their adopted child comes to them in a state of fresh bereavement. He (or she) has just lost not only his mother, but his name, his extended family, his heritage and his genetic history. Just because these infants and children cannot articulate their loss doesn't mean they don't feel it. I believe that if adoptive parents can recognise their child's wound and not react as if she or he lacks appreciation of their adoptive home or loyalty to their adoptive family, there is a greater chance for a close relationship. Listening and allowing and recognising the grief and talking to the child about her loss is the matrix from which a bond can form between parent and child.

Please understand that all of us, adopted or not, need to understand our heritage. To know the names of our parents is our birthright. Regardless of how much love, security and opportunity you have to offer your adopted child, he or she will face unique emotional challenges as they grow up. *These are not your fault and do not reflect poorly on the quality of your parenting.* It is important that you do not underestimate the impact of adoption and that you acknowledge your adopted child's feelings.

Until relatively recently, adopting couples were told to treat the baby just as if it was their own; it would never know the difference. Yet these parents frequently found themselves with babies who didn't bond to them in the way they had hoped. No one understood that babies grieve the loss of their mothers, are likely to have great difficulty in forming attachments to others and are at high risk of addictive behaviour.

Birth mothers were told to get on with their lives; they would forget about their babies; they were doing the right thing; they would be selfish to keep their babies. They were led to believe that they would "get over it". Many women found that this was not possible. They were haunted their whole lives by their decisions and some were never able to marry and have other children.

Second, I hope to educate the general public on the subject of adoption, so that we all have enough awareness to help adopted people and their adoptive families in the trials that adoption can bring.

Third and finally, I hope that my story can help other adopted people who are struggling with anguish that they may not understand. Perhaps you may get something you need from this book and no longer feel alone in your pain. I am glad to say that today so many studies have been done and information is widely available. There are tremendous numbers of support groups and people are beginning to tell the truth and heal their pain. My wish is that anyone involved in adoption will take advantage of all that is available to them. To that end, I have included a resource section at the end of this book, listing publications that have helped me, as well as relevant organisations in the UK.

In addition, the book contains quotations from women who were raised in adoptive homes about the impact of adoption on their lives and, in turn, the impact of motherhood on their adoption issues. They kindly allowed me to interview them about these intimate and frequently painful matters, and I have given them pseudonyms to protect their privacy. Their generosity in sharing their stories is much appreciated.

Zara H Phillips
November 2007

1
In the beginning

*My adoptive mother was infertile; she and my adoptive father
tried for ten years before adopting. I grew up knowing how
emotionally devastating infertility can be.* Yvette

January 1964 was an exciting time in London. The music
scene was bursting wide open with the arrival of the
Beatles, the Rolling Stones, the first broadcasts of Top of
the Pops and great fashion. My birth mother, Patricia, was
sixteen years old. The company she had been working for
as a shorthand typist had moved away and she was enjoying
some free time, hanging out with friends before looking for
another job.

She loved dressing up in all the latest styles and would
spend hours ironing the kinks out of her long dark hair
before going out on the town. A favourite haunt was Les
Enfants Terribles, a club with an upstairs coffee bar and a
dance floor below, where office workers would get
together in their lunch hour for a drink and a dance before
heading back to work. Situated on Wardour Street, in the
heart of Soho, the club was surrounded by Italian
restaurants, making it a popular meeting place for the

many young Italians who came to London in the Sixties to work and learn English. It was here that Pat met my birth father, Vittorio.

She was at the club one lunch time with her friend Valerie, also sixteen but mature for her age and perhaps more experienced at going out and meeting young men. Vittorio, twenty-one years old and working as a waiter, used to come to Les Enfants with a friend during his lunch break and the four started chatting in the coffee bar. They soon paired up and began going out together, often ending up at the Italians' bedsit in Victoria. One evening, a few weeks after they had met, Vittorio took Pat to see a Carry On film. After the movie, they went back to his room and that is when I was conceived.

When I found out after meeting Pat that I had been conceived after one of those Carry On films I wasn't sure what to think. I had loved them as a child but part of me was slightly put out. I couldn't help wondering if those tacky sexy inuendos were what had stimulated my birth parents to get it together. It definitely didn't seem very romantic!

Pat tells me that she knew instantly that she was pregnant but was afraid to tell her parents. As can easily occur when a life event is too overwhelming to assimilate, she pretended it wasn't happening. She remembers reading an article giving information on how to tell if you were pregnant. It said that if you could squeeze a substance from your nipples called colostrum, you were going to have a baby. She tried it and colostrum oozed out. She was terrified. In 1964, nice unwed Jewish girls did not get pregnant, especially by Italian men they barely knew. When Pat told Vittorio the news he responded along the lines of, 'Well, everyone has problems.' Later he called her at home a couple of times but she wouldn't speak to him, a decision she later came to regret.

Patricia and her parents, Jews of Russian, Austrian and

Dutch descent, lived in West London. They were not especially religious and never talked to her about God or spirituality. Particularly, they did not talk to their daughter about sex. In today's tolerant climate, it is impossible for anyone who didn't live through those times to understand the catastrophe of an unplanned pregnancy. It was looked upon as the worst thing a girl could do; it meant that she was morally degenerate and the shame that went with it was crushing. Abortion was illegal and unwed mothers were branded, as many birth mothers have told me, as "spoiled goods".

After Pat became pregnant, she stopped going out. Either her parents didn't notice this dramatic shift or chose not to acknowledge it. Finally, an uncle observed a change in her body and spoke to her mother about his concern. Without discussion, her mother told Pat they were going to see the doctor. She says she just went along with it and once there, the truth came out: Pat was five months pregnant – too far gone for an abortion.

Pat had thought of abortion all along, even though it was illegal. If she had known where to go, she would have had a so-called backstreet abortion without hesitation. Instead, she tried to ignore her situation, hoping that somehow it would just go away.

Once her parents found out, they made all the decisions. Keeping the baby was never considered an option, even though other members of the family were apparently upset about it. It was decided that Pat should go and live with her two uncles for the rest of her pregnancy and that nobody should be told the truth.

No one in the family knew about Pat's condition apart from her mother's married sister, Hilda, and their two brothers, both bachelors who lived together in a flat in Shepherds Bush. The uncles had been involved in Pat's life since she was born and were quite fatherly towards her, so it made sense that she should go to live with them as they had no children of their own. Her father went along with the decision even though he felt the uncles were interfering. Aunt Hilda didn't even tell her husband, and Pat's brother and her friends were informed that she had been offered a job out of London and that she would be gone for a few months.

My birth mother's days in the uncles' flat were long and lonely. She says now that she can't believe she survived it or that she let her parents treat her that way. Nevertheless, uncles and aunt were very loving and supportive. To avoid neighbourhood gossip, Pat was allowed to go outside only at night for fresh air and exercise. Most of her time was spent reading and watching television while the men were at work. Sometimes her mother came to see her.

A few weeks before term, Pat was moved to a home for unmarried mothers. The girls had various jobs, making beds and other light work. Each week, they were visited by a woman from social services who would enquire about their health and answer questions about pregnancy. There was no real discussion of emotional needs or what it would mean to relinquish their babies, or that the decision would forever change their lives. The mothers-to-be were told that giving up their babies was best for the child and that, eventually, they would forget and be able to get on with their lives. Pat told me that, at the time, all she wanted was for everything to be over. She wasn't able to think about the baby. She just wanted her life back. The girls barely talked about their situation, even among themselves; they simply wanted to go home and spent the time listening to the pirate radio station, Radio Caroline. Pat's mother accompanied her to regular check-ups and when she went to the hospital, she was always called Mrs Sampson and had to wear a wedding ring.

On November 4th, Pat went into labour and was transferred to the local hospital, which had a separate building for childbirth. The Annex, as it was known, was situated on Bishop's Avenue, East Finchley. This area of London was known for its beautiful fancy houses and wealthy population. The Annex had once belonged to the film star Gracie Fields. I felt quite glad when I found out that I had arrived in this world on such an opulent street. I recall boasting to my friends, 'Don't you know? I was born on Bishop's Avenue.' My birth mother remembers the building as ornate, with a huge sweeping staircase. It was very unusual for a hospital to be surrounded by such wealth.

Pat's labour was long and difficult. At one point, she cried out to the nurse on duty to help her. The response was, 'You made your bed and you can lie in it,' and the nurse left her to labour alone until the head matron appeared sometime later. The delivery was very hard; she haemorrhaged twice, but I finally arrived in the early morning hours of Guy Fawkes Day, November 5th, 1964.

No one was there to celebrate my birth. Pat remembers hearing fireworks going off before midnight and wondering why London was celebrating so early. When the hospital telephoned her parents, Pat's brother answered the phone and, thinking that he was her father, the nurse informed him of my arrival. Until then he had known nothing. Even after finding out, though, he played along with the secret. He told no one he knew the truth about his sister until I reappeared twenty-four years later.

Apparently, there was a brief discussion about adopting me within the family but that didn't happen. The matron of the hospital told my birth mother that she knew of a German couple who would be interested in adopting me. Pat told her mother, who said that wasn't the way they were going to do it; adoption had to be done through proper channels.

The nurse came round with the paperwork for the birth certificate and asked Pat what the baby's name was. She only had a short time to decide and chose the name Paula.

She had heard the name a few years back and liked it. When her mother heard she had named the baby she was slightly put out. 'You didn't need to be the one that named her,' she said.

After a week in the hospital, Pat was able to take me back to the mother-and-baby home, but the following day she developed an abscess and had to go back. One of the nurses asked where her baby was but Pat didn't know why I hadn't accompanied her. While she was back in hospital – and without her knowledge – I was placed in foster care. By the time she returned to the home I was gone. I remained with my foster carers until January 4th, 1965, when I was taken home by my adoptive parents. Four months later I was legally adopted.

The people who were to become my father and mother had been born and raised in London and were both Jewish. My mother's father was a jeweller and watchmaker who had fought in the First World War and been a Home Guard in the Second. Both he and my grandmother had died before I was born. My adoptive mother often told me about how close they all were and how they enjoyed being together as a family. As I grew older, I found it fascinating that my mother should feel that way towards her parents; such connections were alien to me. I didn't feel like that about anyone and I felt guilty about it.

My parents, Jane and Martin Stanton, spent their childhoods amid the devastation of the Second World War. My father recalls sleeping on the underground train platform, crowded and uncomfortable, along with other Londoners fleeing the air raids above ground. My mother remembers walking home from school and seeing a plane they called a "doodlebug", which was actually a flying bomb. She thought it was following her and she was very frightened. She also recalls watching German and English planes dog-fighting, the name given to duels between aircraft in mid-air. If there was an air raid siren, everyone had to fall to the ground wherever they were.

Jane and Martin met through my mother's cousin Reggie who was at the same university as my father. My mother often used to meet Reggie for lunch and one day he brought along his friend to meet her. A couple of weeks later Reggie invited my mother to a dance. 'Only if you bring your friend,' she said. When he asked my father, the reply was 'Only if you bring your cousin. I don't like dancing and I won't go unless she's there.' Thus began their courtship. Three years later, they became engaged.

My parents got married in September 1954 and were on honeymoon when they found out that my father had successfully passed his apprenticeship to become a solicitor. The beginning of their married life was hard. They lived in a single room with only the barest necessities and received no financial support from either set of parents. Only ten weeks after the wedding, my mother's father died very suddenly. My mother, who had enjoyed an especially close relationship to him, was devastated. At the same time, my father was up for his turn at national service, which was compulsory in many European countries at that time. Any day, he could be called up for as long as three years, so no one wanted to give him a job. This actually turned out to be the proverbial blessing in disguise, since it forced my father to open his own practice, which eventually became hugely successful.

As the practice began to thrive and they were able to afford more comforts and amenities, I'm sure my parents believed that the next stage would be to start their own family. Jane had always loved and wanted children, and although we have discussed it only briefly, I can only imagine their disappointment and grief when they found out it was not possible.

They decided to adopt and their rabbi put them in touch with an adoption society in the heart of London. They had to produce various documents and explanations of why they wanted to have a child; they had to be interviewed in their home to make sure they would be acceptable parents. One requirement was photographs of not only themselves but of their parents, along with descriptions of hair and eye colour so that they could be matched with a baby who bore a general resemblance to them. Since they were Jewish, they were told they could adopt only a Jewish baby. My mother was upset and asked why the baby had to be Jewish. 'Adopted children have many problems, and to give you a child of a different faith would only add to them,' was the reply. There was no guarantee that a baby would ever become available to them, as Jewish babies weren't so easy to come by.

Happily, nine months after they applied, they were asked if they wanted to adopt my brother, Graham. They agreed straight away. When my brother was two-and-a-half, they received confirmation that there was a baby girl for them. She was the last Jewish baby the adoption society had and my parents were thrilled. This time, they waited eight months, and the main photograph the agency wanted to see was of Graham, to make sure we would look alike.

I am not quite sure what photos the agency was looking at in relation to my mother and I resembling one another as we really didn't match at all: my mother has always had blonde hair, a rounded figure and creamy white skin; I have almost black hair and a very slim build with olive skin that tans a deep brown. My father, on the other hand, had black hair, as did my adopted brother. There the similarities between us end.

In Judaism, it is the mother's line that determines whether the child is Jewish. (Paternity may be questionable, but maternity never is.) Patricia's mother had to show the adoption agency her marriage certificate to demonstrate that her husband had got married in a synagogue, proving that I had a Jewish line from the mother's side. The fact that my birth father was Italian and most likely Roman Catholic held no relevance for my adoptive parents. I had a Jewish mother and that was all that mattered. And so I joined their family. My adoption was finalised on April 6th, 1965 and my new birth certificate was registered with my new name.

My father continued to work hard in his practice and when I was thirteen years old he became a district judge. He travelled each day to the city and provided a comfortable life for his family. Like many fathers of that generation, he had little involvement in raising his children. He kept to himself, working hard to pay for our education and, I believe, getting all the information he wanted about my brother and I from my mother.

We saw quite a lot of my paternal grandparents. I have memories of my grandfather saying to me at dinnertime, 'Eat your greens. It'll make your hair grow!' I'd always laugh, as my hair grew nearly to my waist. He was a kind man, but seemed to exist in the shadow of my grandmother who spoke without thinking, smoked constantly and (so I am told) gambled away his money whenever she had the opportunity. She was a great source of irritation to my grandfather just by being herself. I have many vivid memories of sitting around the table when they came to Sunday lunch, which happened most weekends.

Sunday was the only day of the week when we all sat opposite each other and ate together as a family. The rest of the week, we sat in a row, like birds on a fence, along one side of our long green kitchen table in order to watch TV while we ate. Everyone had a great view except for me. I used to be on the far right end and couldn't see a thing except the dining-room table and chairs. Whenever I protested and asked to be moved, my parents seemed annoyed. I could never understand why my brother got the best seat. I would sit quietly, but after a while would feel a stirring from way low in my stomach, a mass of anger and frustration that felt ready to burst. These feelings were becoming all too familiar, but I didn't know how to manage or control them. I ate as fast as I could.

On Sundays, though, the TV was turned off and we sat around the table. I had a great view of my grandparents. I would listen to my grandmother make a statement about someone and watch my grandfather begin to shrink into his seat, muttering under his breath. 'You would think that,' he'd say or start tutting. There was lots of tutting whenever my grandmother spoke. I knew she had upset my parents many times, but I was never told exactly what she had done. I did know, however, that she had never been forgiven nor was likely to be. She often angered my grandfather with her selfishness and outspoken ways, but I found her amusing. I also felt sorry for her, as I could tell that sometimes she was simply making a joke. But nobody found her funny and they would take any opportunity to show their irritation.

When I became a teenager and started smoking cigarettes, my grandmother was positively joyful. She would often say, 'Zara, let's go and have a smoke,' and off we'd go down the road. As we chatted about this and that, she would hand out cigarette after cigarette until I felt quite sick. A good few years later she offered me one as always and I declined, telling her that I had finally given up. Her face dropped. 'Really, are you sure? Oh go on. Have one of mine.'

'Grandma,' I said, explaining my huge withdrawal from cigarettes, 'You're meant to be helping me.'

'Are you sure you don't want just one more?' she urged.

'Grandma,' I said loudly 'You're my grandmother. You're supposed to be pleased.'

I felt a connection with her, a fondness that still remains with me, although she passed away in March 2002. At the same time, my father's emotional distance caused me hurt and confusion. My mother said it was because he was shy and I had to accept that about him but, as a young girl, I took it extremely personally and felt it as a huge rejection.

Sometimes I'd try to talk to him and he would just stare at the ground as if I wasn't there. I couldn't understand why and would feel the tears burning in my eyes and a tightening of my heart. The worst part, though, was the feeling of self-hatred that had begun to take hold.

My mother worked with my father but managed to juggle being at home with us. She was a great homemaker and cook and often wanted me to watch her, to prepare me to be a good Jewish wife. But cooking held no interest for me. I would stand next to her yawning as loudly as I could as she explained how to make matzo ball soup, and when I took it upon myself to make a sandwich she would hold up the loaf to demonstrate how crooked I had cut the bread into slices like doorsteps.

She was very involved in our lives and did her best to please us and be a loving mother. Unlike her husband, she has always been a gregarious woman; she adores people and loves to talk. What I really wanted was for her to read my mind, to understand why I was the way I was . . . but she never did. Our family was complete and adoption was rarely mentioned.

2
The good adoptee

I have always carried guilt that I've done something wrong, and I spent a lot of my relationships apologising. Then I finally had my son and I realised that he couldn't make a mistake at his age. When I met my birth mother she told me that I had done nothing wrong. That was very powerful. Wendy

We lived in Totteridge, a suburb in North London, and although it is not too far out from London itself, it was almost like living in the country. It had one long, winding main road surrounded by grassy mounds and dirt tracks that mostly led to large eighteenth-century houses. When I was a child, there was also a small farm where my mother often took me to buy fresh eggs and milk.

Totteridge has an interesting history and is listed in *The Domesday Book*. Once for school I had to do a project on the history of where I lived. I discovered that the name Totteridge is Anglo-Saxon, and that over the centuries it had been spelled in at least eight different ways, including Taterig and Tattyridge. I also learned that in 1946, a Bronze-Age chisel had been found in a street near our house, and that Julius Caesar had passed through

Totteridge in 54 BC. I enjoyed knowing that Queen Elizabeth I had owned Totteridge Manor in 1562. In fact, anything with a plaque dating back so long ago held my immediate interest. I wanted to know the stories of what I called 'the real people' behind it. I would imagine them walking on the very streets and land that I stood on. Maybe I grasped onto others' history because I felt the void of my own.

Totteridge had one bus, the notorious 251, that never seemed to arrive on time. If you missed it, you could sit for up to an hour waiting for another. On the days when I decided it would be quicker to walk, I could be sure that as soon as I was in between bus stops, a red 251 would whiz by. Sometimes I ran as fast as I could to catch it at the next stop, yelling to get the driver's attention, but more often than not the driver never even slowed down. My journey up Totteridge Lane would have to be completed on foot. On those days, I looked lovingly and longingly at the old houses and wished that our family lived in one of them instead of the modern single-storey bungalow that my parents proudly had had designed and built for them in the Sixties.

I had always wanted a home with stairs and different floors. Our house featured a long corridor, with doors on either side leading to our bedrooms. I was scared of that corridor, especially when all the doors were shut. My dad would yell out to turn the light off before I had even reached my room. This became a constant argument, since the light switch was at one end of the corridor and my room was in the middle. How was I supposed to get there in the dark? I tried to explain it over and over again, but my father had this fixation about turning off lights to avoid running up a huge bill. I tried various methods of getting to my room, sometimes in the dark, just feeling my way along the wall, my heart beating and my anxious hands convinced I was going to come into contact with some slimy object – or worse, someone's body – before I reached my sanctuary. Once I found my door and then the light switch, I would be so relieved that I would shut the door as quickly as possible without looking back into the dark void. The other option was to hear my dad yelling, 'Turn off the light!' as I ran as fast as I could to my bedroom. I'd fling the door wide, turn on the light so that it spilled into the corridor, then run back and turn off the corridor light. It all depended on how I was feeling that evening.

The other inconvenience about our house was that the front door led straight into the TV room. You had to walk past my parents sitting on the sofa, which some of my friends found terrifying. My dad, who would only mutter a hello, was especially daunting. Embarrassed by his quiet ways, I'd hustle my friends through the corridor as fast as I could so we could get to the refuge of my bedroom.

I stayed what they call the "good adoptee" for quite a while, keeping my feelings to myself, while I watched my brother go through a difficult time. Well before reaching his teens, Graham would bring up the subject of adoption in anger and tears. He would say all the stuff that I wanted to say, like, 'You are not my real mother,' and 'I want to find her.' He showed his rage but I saw how much it hurt our mother's feelings, so, from an early age, it became my job to protect everyone. I felt that I had to hide from them that I too was angry. I couldn't be honest. I thought I owed it to my mother not to behave like him, but it didn't last long.

Graham and I often called each other names. I suppose most siblings do, but the word *bastard* was always loaded for us.

'You're such a bastard,' I would say.

'But so are you,' he'd reply.

'But I am not a bastard any more,' I responded in defence.

'Once a bastard, always a bastard,' he'd fired back.

Then I would run to my mother and ask her if I really

was a bastard, which my brother found hysterically funny. My poor mother. I could see her flinch when I said the word. It wasn't easy for her to know how to answer. I remember her saying, 'Hmm umm, well no, you are not now because you are adopted.'

I would persist, part of me wanting her to acknowledge it, since being illegitimate wasn't common at the time and, in a strange way, it made me feel interesting and different. 'But Mum,' I would say. 'I was born a bastard so I must be one!'

'Oh Zara, well, yes but . . .'

Back then, people still lived with the Victorian belief that if you were born a bastard, you were no good, stupid, not fit to live. Films about earlier times just reinforced the view that you deserved very little if you were a "bastard child". Even at school, as we learned about historical figures, it seemed essential to mention if they were bastards.

Naturally, all this was extremely confusing and conflicting for me. I felt drawn to whichever character or celebrity or writer that critics made sure to point out was a bastard. I always felt some identification with these people and was secretly glad to hear of their successes. It was a strange dichotomy: how could I tell anyone that I felt like a bastard and understood these characters' struggles to succeed, their need for recognition? People believed that the word *adoption* took away the stigma and, along with it, the need to know your birth family.

Nevertheless, these consolations never worked and I realise today that I believed all those subtle and not-so-subtle messages. I believed I was less intelligent than others, that somehow my brain didn't work in the same way.

Then, of course, there was God and religion. Was I worthy of God's love? Was it my fault that I had been born this way? Had I done something dreadful in a past life? I knew one thing: I had better make sure I told God how grateful I was for being alive, and be sure to pray extra hard to make up for being a bastard so that I, too, could feel God's acceptance. This was tricky because, at the same time, I was extremely angry with this loving God who made sure I was given up for adoption. I was convinced for a long while it was because I had been bad.

So *bastard* became great ammunition for my brother and me to taunt each other. Sometimes we laughed and other times we were extremely sensitive. That was our way of talking about adoption.

I often spent time thinking about what my mother's biological daughter would have been like if she had had her own child, especially when I was having a difficult time with her. I would imagine this daughter looking like my mother, with a round figure like a lot of the Jewish girls I knew. Of course, she would have loved everything that my mother loved and I didn't – she'd be happy to accompany her to fundraising events at the synagogue, to join the Jewish club for boys and girls and be friends with "suitable people" – all the things that made me feel so uncomfortable and that I felt guilty for not wanting to do. I could almost feel this daughter's presence in our house. Her shadow somehow hung around me, following me. I felt I knew her personality, what she looked like and how she thought of me as the intruder in her home.

3
Hidden truths

Every day since I learned I was adopted, in 1996 when my son was four, I stare at people who are biologically related to each other. It amazes me; people must think I am an idiot to be so floored that relatives look alike. Clara

After school, practically every day, I would hurry across the street to my girlfriends' house. Katie, Roberta and I had known each other since we were babies and, as we grew older, we became inseparable. I loved being with them. I so wanted to be their sister and we were close enough to pretend we were. I could see the connection between them, the similarities that made them family. I often felt great sadness because I knew that, no matter how close we were, I wasn't their sister. When I left their house to go home in the evening, I'd feel an emptiness, a feeling that always took hold of me once I was alone.

By the time I was about twelve years old, I became aware that not all babies who were adopted were of the same religion or culture as their adoptive parents. That really bothered me. I couldn't believe that some children didn't know their origins and grew afraid that my parents were keeping something from me. A few days after first experiencing this realisation, I was standing in the kitchen with my mother. She had her back to me and was busy making supper. I mustered up all my courage and asked in a small voice, 'Was my birth mother Jewish?' Jane assured me that she was, and I said, 'But how do you know? Was my birth father Jewish too? Am I really Jewish?'

My mother repeated, 'Yes, you are Jewish,' but she never turned to look at me. I knew then, staring at her back, that there was something she wasn't telling me. Her answer just didn't sit right in my soul, but at that time, I was still too afraid to ask more for fear of upsetting her. It was another twelve years before I found out that my birth father was Italian and that my parents had known this all along.

I was told that it wasn't necessary to let everyone know I was adopted. I never understood why because I always wanted to tell people. One day at school I was walking into my classroom when I heard some girls talking about me. I stopped quickly by the door so they couldn't see me and listened.

'She's adopted,' I heard one of them say.

'Is she really?' said another voice.

'It's true. Isn't it sad?' replied the first girl.

At that point, I made my grand entrance and the girls looked up. 'I don't mind you knowing I am adopted. You can ask me any questions, or when you come over, you can talk to my mother. She knows more about it than me.' I felt extremely important, so when my friends came over to my house, I told my mother that they needed to talk to her about my adoption. She said she would be happy to and I heard my friend say, 'Is she really adopted?' Then I left them to it. I don't really know why; I felt it would be easier for them to be honest if I wasn't there, so I went outside and sat on the wall feeling in some ways quite important and hopeful that my friends might somehow understand how I felt. My mother never mentioned the conversation and I didn't ask.

One afternoon, my brother and I were standing at the front door with my mother and some of her friends. The husband gazed at me intently. 'Who does she look like then? I think it's her dad.' They looked at my tall, skinny, olive-skinned body and dark brown hair and then at my blonde adoptive mother and her shapely figure. 'Yes,' the man concluded, 'she really looks like Martin.' My mother readily agreed.

I stayed silent but I wanted so desperately to say, 'I am adopted.' The glance that came from my mother, though, made me feel it wouldn't be the right thing. I felt annoyed until Graham spoke up, 'It's pure coincidence, I can assure you.' At that point we looked at each other and cracked up laughing. The poor man didn't know what he had said and Mother hurried him out the door.

As a child, I could never fit into my bed, not because it was too small but because I had so many teddy bears lined up next to me there was only a tiny space for me to squeeze in next to them. I loved my teddies and was very attached to them. I even remember writing nametags for them all so that when my babysitter came over she would know who they each were when it was time to kiss them goodnight.

I suffered silently from compulsive behaviour. For instance, my teddies all had to have partners so they wouldn't feel lonely and I had to do everything twice. This became very annoying and would often delay my leaving the house or getting ready for the day. Some days, I found myself eating the same food twice so that the food had company, or I walked endlessly back and forth across my room. Sometimes I sat in my room and felt the walls closing in around me as if I was being suffocated. Even at a young age, I sensed that my behaviour wasn't quite normal and that if I revealed myself they might consider locking me away.

When I was about twelve, I was invited to spend a week

in Spain with a school friend and her family. I wanted very much to accept and thought I was grown up enough to go abroad. The day before we were due to leave, I stayed the night at their house and lay awake in the dark, gripped with that familiar fear I always had when I was away from home. I knew then I had made a dreadful mistake.

I spent the entire week in Spain in my bedroom. My friend and her parents tried to coax me out, but I would cry and shake and wait for my mother to call me from London. I needed the reassurance of her voice to calm what I can only describe as a rising panic. I wanted to go home, but was told by my hosts that I should stay and enjoy myself, that I would be OK. I did have one rare moment of being able to relax with the family when the mother turned to me in the car and said, 'You know Zara, you are really good company and fun to be with.' I was shocked. No one had ever said that to me before.

I was embarrassed by my behaviour and scared that my friend would tell everyone at school and I would be made fun of. But the fear crippled me and I stayed in the bedroom. I wrote in my diary that I was adopted and that I was very lucky to have my family, that I loved them very much and I knew they loved me. 'Being adopted hasn't affected me at all,' I wrote, 'I am so lucky to have been adopted and not put in an orphanage.' I drew hearts around my family's names. When it was time to go back to London, I was so relieved, but when I got home, my brother made fun of me and my mother couldn't understand what had been wrong. I was devastated.

Every time I stayed at someone's house, a parent would end up hearing me cry in the night and try to comfort me. I'd end up going home, ashamed that I wasn't able to stay away even a single night. I had no control over the feelings that surfaced – mainly intense fear. I believed that if I was away from my family they would die, but as long as I could see them, everything would be OK. I never told anyone about these fears, believing that if I did, they would think me silly.

I have always loved babies and young children. Even as a child, if ever the opportunity arose to take care of a baby, I did it eagerly. A particular incident came back to me only recently. One Jewish holiday when I was ten or eleven, my family and I spent the day in synagogue (holidays were usually the only times we observed our religion) and I played all day with a small child. I had lots of energy and I enjoyed being in charge. After the service the family asked me if I would like to come back to their house and have dinner. My parents could collect me later or my hosts would drive me home. With my parents' permission, I readily agreed.

I felt quite shy but the family was so welcoming. The mother was glowingly pregnant with her second child and her husband very warm and loving. They both talked to me easily, including me in their conversations. When we sat down to dinner, some other family members joined us. I sat opposite the mother and watched the candles in the middle of the table and listened to the prayers and blessings. Suddenly, I felt very sad and began to cry. I wanted to go home. I tried to hide my emotions as best I could, but she soon noticed. She took me out of the room and asked me gently what was wrong, but I didn't know. I just wanted to go home.

4
Fantasy

Being a mother made me think much more often about being adopted. I had always accepted the fact that I was adopted. I was raised knowing that she [my birth mother] did the best thing for me at the time. But once my children were here, I kept finding myself wishing that I knew who she was and where she was, wondering if she was thinking about me. There were nights I would lie in bed and in my head I would scream out for her to contact me. The pain was horrible. Laurel

As a child, I had always had the desire to express myself. At the age of eight, I began to write stories. They were mainly adventure fantasies and as soon as I had finished one, I would go to the kitchen and read them to my mother while she cooked. I also began to read more. I identified keenly with Dickens's character, Oliver Twist, which was confusing. After all, I had a mother, hadn't I? I wasn't an orphan. I subsequently found myself writing about disabilities and overcoming them. One of my stories was entered into a competition at school. I remember the teacher saying, 'What an unusual topic for a girl of your age!'

Music was another great passion. Some days I couldn't wait to close the door to my bedroom and listen to a new record, usually a musical I had heard about. If I couldn't get the songbook I would spend hours listening to the record, taking the needle off the disc after each line so that I could write out the lyrics. Completing a single song could take half an hour, but once I had all the words I could do the truly exhilarating part, the performance, where I played all the parts and sang all the songs. My only audience was my dolls and teddies, who always watched appreciatively as I lost myself in the emotion and beauty of words and music. Sometimes I pictured my birth mother sitting in a chair, smiling proudly at me.

I always had the feeling that I was being watched, as if I was part of some experiment. I would find myself showing off to these "people", talking to them and feeling a certain comfort in their presence. Of course I had no idea who they were, but I was convinced of their presence nonetheless.

It was strangely comforting. At those times, I felt a connection to something yet I couldn't explain what. I only knew that when I finished singing the connection was lost.

I felt ugly a lot of the time. I didn't see myself as a normal, pretty little girl because inside I felt defective. Everyone else was better than I was. I found it almost impossible to stop the self-hatred, the voice that repeated how silly I was when I made a mistake and the constant fear that people would reject me.

I fantasised a lot about my birth mother. I looked for her on the streets; it was just part of what I did as an adopted person. Some people looked at trees or flowers, I looked at women's faces and wondered if I would recognise her or she me. Who was I? Where was I from? Was I English? Jewish? Really, what was the truth? On the other hand, I was scared to know because I also carried the belief common to adopted people that the mother who had given me away would never be interested in meeting me.

Sometimes I woke in the morning and imagined that this was the day she would come and collect me. I would spend the whole day believing that she was about to arrive, peering out of the window in the hope of seeing her. I would fantasise about opening the front door, looking her straight in the eye and deciding whether to invite her in or merely slam the door in her face. Often I dreamed about her, but when it came time for me to look at her face, it was always blank.

I spent much of my time in my head daydreaming and never really feeling connected with anyone. But secretly I was always waiting for the day that Mother would show up on my doorstep, apologising and telling me there had been a terrible mistake.

When I had arguments with my family or friends, I took everything so personally, so deeply, that I couldn't feel at peace until things had been resolved. I never wanted anyone to know the depths of my insecurity, nor could I really explain what was going on inside me. As I grew older, my difficulties grew bigger and more out of control.

Paradoxically, feeling connected to anyone was incredibly frightening, yet connection was what I craved most. I tried many things to fill the inner emptiness, which felt like it would devour me if I didn't anaesthetise it in some way. When I was ten or eleven, I went through a phase of always making sure I came home with a present for everyone in the family – even the dog – when I went out shopping with my friends. My mother told me I didn't need to spend my pocket money on them, but I couldn't buy myself a gift unless I made sure I had something for my parents. I needed their approval, but mostly I needed to know they were going to keep me.

My mother had a large suitcase filled with photographs of her parents and relatives. There were also letters that my parents wrote to each other, along with birthday cards dating back to before I was born and some from when my brother and I were small.

The soft brown leather was musty and scuffed with age, yet I loved that old suitcase. Even though the lock was broken, it still managed to contain everything. I often asked my mother if we could look through it. She was always happy to oblige and would stand on a stool to reach up into her bedroom cupboard and take it down. I would help her lower it to the floor, and then we would sit on the carpet and explore the contents.

I especially enjoyed finding anything having to do with me and my brother, such as early photos, birthday cards or medical cards. I would ask my mother to identify everybody in the old black-and-white photos and to tell me how we were related. I always looked intently at those faces. I so wanted to feel connected to them, to really feel that they were my relatives, yet I always found myself wondering what my birth family looked like. I thought of the people in the photos as my mother's relatives.

I began to search my parents' belongings when they were away from home. As soon as they left the house, I would go through drawers and files to see what I could find. I never consciously knew what I was looking for. Perhaps they had a secret, maybe my parents weren't who they said they were. Maybe they were lying to me about my adoption, or things were a lot worse than they had told me. Perhaps I wasn't really adopted at all. I went through the same drawers time after time, convinced I had missed something. I never did find anything remarkable, but I never stopped trying. Even at night when I was meant to be in bed, I snooped around the house. I'd cram my ear to their bedroom door to try and hear what my parents were talking about: maybe they would mention me and reveal something I didn't know. I didn't realise until years later that it was information about myself that I was looking for.

I knew very early on that I was adopted. I have no

memory of when I was actually told. I just remember a book on adoption that was read to me. There was a roomful of babies lined up in their cribs and a couple walked along, examining each one. There was one baby who didn't smile and was 'far too serious for them'. They said he wasn't the right one and they finally decided on a cute, happy, chubby baby, who was 'exactly the kind of baby they wanted'. The book invariably left me with a feeling of deep sadness. What, I wondered, happened to the serious baby? Who took him home to love?

I could never express my feelings to anyone. I often heard my family say, 'Zara is just so moody.' I became very angry when I heard that and also extremely depressed. It wasn't as though I liked being moody, yet I couldn't change it on my own and I didn't know why.

I believe my parents wanted to think of us as their very own. My father has never mentioned adoption and my mother talked about it only in answer to my questions – she never brought it up first. I longed for her to ask me how I felt about my birth mother, or to tell me that my birth mother had been pretty and good. I yearned for some scrap of history, for my own story. Their lack of acknowledgment made me furious and confused. Perhaps they were advised not to bring up the issue of adoption, but the message I got was that adoption was taboo. Consequently, I was extremely fearful of bringing it up. It took me days or weeks to work up my courage. I tried to ignore my pounding heart, which beat faster and faster as I waited for an opportune moment to speak up. Then, for fear that my mother would be upset when she truly saw my desperation, I spoke in a small, off-hand voice that I thought conveyed only cool interest. Her usual response was, 'Your mother was young.' I tried to look casual, when in reality I was concentrating hard so as to not miss one word of information.

5
A yearning to connect

I didn't know I was adopted until I was twenty-seven. I felt absolutely connected to my baby – he was the only thing I could feel connected to, even though I was unaware of my adoption status. I didn't feel a connection to anyone nor did I resemble anyone [in my family]. Continuity seemed to be non-existent. Martha

I had always thought about my birth mother but it wasn't until I started a new school and headed towards puberty that I began to feel the differences between me and my peers. I was in a private all girls' school with the full uniform, which we would adapt to make ourselves stand out from one another. We had blue shirts, ties, blazers and indoor and outdoor shoes. Depending on the fashion, my plain school skirt went from being extremely short to very long and tight; underneath we would have to wear brown woollen knickers that were so big on my skinny body that I could pull them up to under my armpits, creating an extra layer in winter that kept me warm, much to the envy of some of the larger girls.

Relationships between my schoolmates were quite

intense. I began to become more aware of my body, especially when we had to change for gym. Other girls would point out that I was skinny and had no breasts, even at twelve, and they wondered if I ever would. The girls talked about their bodies and compared them with those of their mothers. 'That's why I have fat thighs,' my friend said. 'I didn't stand a chance; it runs in my family. All the women have fat thighs.'

I always laughed along with the others, unable, though, to participate in the conversation. In my silence I wondered what I had in common with my birth mother. I would stare at my friends and their siblings, taking in the family resemblance and feel the gap that separated me from them. I didn't fit in. I hadn't been born like them; in fact, I didn't know how I had been born. I didn't have a birth story. I wanted to know if my mother craved chocolate or oranges when she was pregnant, whether I was a week early or late, what I looked like when I was born. When a school friend told me some details about her birth, I was genuinely interested.

At the end of the school day we would all scramble to the small mirror in the corridor and put on our make-up before walking past the boys' school up the road. I spent a lot of time looking in the mirror. I had no idea what I really looked like, although the headmistress did comment once that the purple lipstick I was wearing made me look as if I had frostbite.

I felt as though I had to lie about my adoptive status and pretend that none of it mattered because I didn't want, at any cost, to hurt my adoptive parents or for them to not know how grateful I was that they had chosen me. Nor could I reveal to anyone the real belief I carried – that I must have been bad somewhere along the line or extremely ugly and defective because, unlike my friends, my mother had given me away.

I always had the feeling that I should be happy. After all,

I had everything: a nice house, clothes, I went to a good school and I had lots of friends. I wanted to believe the story of what other people thought of adoption, that I was "special" because I had been "chosen" and I was really wanted. When my mother read me the story of adoption, I tried so hard to be happy about it, not understanding why I wasn't. I didn't want to hurt her by asking too many questions, so I began to protect my family from my true feelings. I was scared of their reaction, their pain, but most importantly, I didn't want to be rejected.

In my class at school I had a good friend, Nikki, who was also adopted. We would talk about our situation and feelings and it was a great source of comfort and connection for me. When we were fourteen, we decided to take the day off school and go up to town to see what we could find out about our birth mothers.

We planned the day. Our parents dropped us off at school, as they did each day, but instead of going into the building we met outside, hiding behind the cars parked along the narrow tree-lined street. Our school was a large Victorian house, nestled in greenery, with a small dirt car park that stood halfway up a hill. The hill led down past a graveyard to some sweetshops. We'd run through the graveyard and shin up a wall onto a concrete slab that levered us up onto the shop roof. From there, we found our way down between the buildings so we could go and buy our sweets and cigarettes.

We chose to walk up the hill, where we wouldn't be visible from the school windows. The road wound past a triangular plot of grass with a medium-sized pond. Alongside the pond lay a row of small terraced houses that dated back to the eighteenth century. The tiny doors reminded us of how much smaller people had been back then. I thought they were wonderful and wanted so much to live in one of them.

We ran up the hill, ducking and diving behind parked

cars. Once we were past the pond, we knew we were out of sight of the school and only had to worry about teachers and pupils driving past and seeing us going in the opposite direction. We sneaked down a side street, past the boys' school and onto a red bus that took us to a tube station. We hadn't thought of changing clothes to make us less conspicuous, so we were still dressed in our school uniforms with the school emblem embroidered on the front of our blazers for all to see.

We headed for the heart of London, to the Births, Marriages and Deaths Office at Catherine House. We giggled a lot on the train, making jokes about who our birth mothers might be and became quite hysterical, as only teenage girls can, causing a few raised eyebrows among our fellow passengers. We found Catherine House along the crowded streets and entered through a revolving door that led straight to the receptionist. Instantly our bravado faded in the bureaucratic atmosphere.

I let Nikki do the talking. She always seemed to come across as more grown up than me and I thought we would stand a better chance of being taken seriously. Nikki told the receptionist we were doing a project for school, and she directed us to where the adoption birth certificates were located. I felt butterflies in my stomach and my breathing grew shallow as we entered the room. I looked at Nikki. 'I feel sick,' she said. I nodded in agreement.

We were both scared, but we went ahead anyway to look up our dates of birth. I found my adoption birth certificate easily. It gave only my adopted name and my adoptive parents' names: Jane and Martin Stanton. Nothing else. I don't quite know what I had expected to find but I felt relief, in part, I think, because I could be sure that at least that element of my history was true.

I heard Nikki from across the room. 'Oh, my God!' She had found another girl with her exact name, born a year before her birthday. For a split second, she thought that she might be younger than she was, but she soon found herself in the records. I sensed her relief.

By that point, she seemed to be as ready as I was to leave. Back on the street, we looked at each other. Now what? We had picked up a pamphlet on obtaining adoption records that included a phone number. We decided to call and see what happened.

We both huddled in the phone box and I got Nikki to speak in her grown-up way while I whispered instructions on what she should say. She wasn't on the phone long. The lady at the other end asked how old we were and suggested that maybe we ought to discuss this with our parents or wait a little while till we were older. Nikki put down the phone. We lingered in the phone box, our moods darkening.

'You hungry?' I asked at last.

'Yes,' she replied. Off we went to have lunch.

6
Acting out

I know my son looks 'just like me' from others' comments, but because I was a different race from my adopters, I always thought I was hideously ugly. **Adrian**

As I approached my teens, my brother and I switched roles. He began to take drugs and appeared more reasonable (when in fact he was stoned), and I began to vent my anger, which increasingly deepened into rage. My mother and I began to argue constantly until screaming and yelling at each other became part of the daily routine. My moods depended on whether or not I had something to look forward to, such as a party or a new boyfriend. But as soon as the party was over or the boyfriend was out of the picture, I would spiral down once again into deep depression. Sometimes I snorted speed or cocaine to lift my mood. I didn't know what I was angry about. All I knew was that I felt bad nearly all the time, really bad. If anyone noticed, they didn't know what to do. Neither did I.

Often I sought refuge in the local church and cemetery. I loved to walk among the old gravestones and read the inscriptions, then find their relatives buried nearby. I was especially drawn to the section where infants and children lay. I worried that their headstones were too small and that they wouldn't be remembered. Inside the church, I experienced the peace and calm that only a place of prayer brings. As I reached my fourteenth year, the church became an essential place for me to go and smoke a much-needed cigarette, my first drug. I would tell my mother I was going for a run. I would run until I came to the church where I could sit quietly, hidden from the main street, and feel my heart beat faster in anticipation of taking that first drag. With it came the instant relaxation of every fibre of my being. Aahhh, I felt so much better!

On the way home, I'd chew gum, convinced that it would take away any lingering smell. If my mother guessed my secret vice, she never said a word. In fact if Jane ever knew anything I was doing that wasn't in my best interest, she never let on.

Our picturesque local pub, The Orange Tree, had a pond with ducks and geese. I learned to fear those birds; once, I took my friend's little brother to feed them, but he wouldn't let go of the bread, and the geese started chasing him. All I could think of was to shout at the geese and tell him to run. I was too scared for my own safety to rescue him. When I was a teenager that pond became a source of great laughs. My friends and I would go to the pub on winter evenings. We were too young to go in, so we had to sit outside freezing, begging the older boys to get us a drink. My girlfriend, who had recently passed her driving test, managed somehow to reverse her car into the pond and got her wheels stuck. And of course there was always the threat of being thrown into the murky water by some drunk.

After our nights at The Orange Tree, I often had to walk home. The old church and cemetery that I so loved in the daytime felt very different in the dark. No matter how much I tried to not look into the grounds, I couldn't help myself. I could swear I saw things moving among the headstones and I'd end up running as fast as I could down the little lane to the top of our street, where I felt safe again. My parents didn't know I walked back from the pub so often. They thought Graham had taken me there on the back of his motorcycle or dropped me home. Usually he said, 'Find your own way home, I'm busy.' Then I would see some long-haired blonde jump on the back and ride off with him, her arms tight around his waist and him beaming like a Cheshire cat, revving the engine extra loudly so everyone would turn to look at him. I would roll my eyes in disgust and feel mad that she got to hold him by the waist – I was never allowed to.

It's strange to grow up with someone who is your brother when you both know that genetically you are not related at all, that you both have different parents and there's a strong chance you have real siblings somewhere in the world, who probably look very much like you. My relationship with Graham had a tremendous impact on my life. As a young boy, he was extremely withdrawn, staying in his room away from people as much as possible. I, on the other hand, had lots of friends and liked to socialise. From an early age, my brother had various behavioural problems; he often stole things and would bully me and anyone around him. By the time he was a teenager he was caught with a huge variety of goods he had accumulated. I remember sitting outside his bedroom door as my mother asked him to remove all the stolen items he had and out he came, carrying piles of records, a record player, speakers . . . I sat there in disbelief. (I've since learned that stealing is a known syndrome of adopted children who often feel stolen themselves.)

As he grew into his teens, my brother changed a lot and began to make himself be noticed by shaving his head and piercing his ear, which at the time was quite shocking. I remember seeing Graham smoke marijuana for the first time. He allowed me into his room, a privilege I dared not refuse. I sat on the bed and watched attentively as he rolled a joint and smoked it. My response to watching him inhale was as if I had smoked it myself: I felt as though an electrical current had rushed through my body. I was extremely scared, yet I was exhilarated by a rush of excitement. At that moment, I knew my life was about to change. Anything could happen.

The progression of drug addiction is not pleasant to watch. It's odd how easy it is to see it in others but not in yourself. For many years, my focus was on Graham. I became consumed by his every move and diligent about lying for him to protect his supply for fear that he really would kill me or hurt me even more than he was already doing. Our house became the meeting place for all our friends and the people Graham hung out with would be taking heroin or snorting cocaine and smoking joints. These activities became a normal part of everyday life. I loved seeing some of my brother's friends. They were almost three years older than me and I would hope in vain that I'd be invited into his room.

When I was feeling confident, I would just march in and sit down and chat with Graham's friends and he'd let me stay for a while. But most of the time I would open the door a crack and my brother would yell, 'Get out, you slut!' or '. . . you tart.' If I was lucky I would get away without any physical damage. Emotionally, though, I was always bruised, yet I just kept repeating my behaviour, knowing each time that I was putting myself at risk.

By this time, my parents had bought a flat some distance away, where they often spent long weekends, not knowing that Graham's addiction had now taken full control. As usual, I remained silent, thinking that somehow I could manage.

The parties started the moment my parents left and went on until the big clean-up moments before their return. All our friends would come over and the drugs would begin. My brother became a bully to everyone present and I felt more and more ashamed of him, and wished I wasn't connected to him in any way. Yet when the friends had gone home and I found Graham in a drug-induced sleep in front of a blank, beeping TV screen, I would look at his pale face and dark eyes, knowing that he really wasn't a violent bully – he was just as frightened and lost as I was.

I would sometimes drag him to bed or at least throw a blanket over him and pray that he would live till the next day. Once in my own bed, I'd try to sleep, but eventually I would go back to his room just to make sure he was still breathing. Only then could I settle myself. I knew I ought to tell my parents and yet I was terrified. Graham had made me promise not to say anything. The truth was that I desperately wanted him to like me. I also needed to feel connected to him. We both had a lot of healing to do and, although we didn't know it at the time, we couldn't help each other. At the same time, there was an unspoken understanding between us: we were both adopted and we could understand each other in a way our friends couldn't.

When I was nineteen, the manager of the restaurant where we both worked noticed Graham's problem and took it upon himself to tell my parents. By then, Graham had been a heroin addict for three years. I remember my mother asking why I hadn't told her. I could barely answer. 'I tried,' I whispered.

My brother was immediately sent to a treatment centre and, from then on, spent several years involved in various recovery programmes. While Graham was first away, my mother decided she wanted to paint his room. She asked me to help her go through everything, because she felt that when he came out of treatment, it would be nice for him to come home to a fresh start. As it was, the bedroom was painted almost black and the curtains were yellow from all the smoking. It was hard to believe that the rest of the house we lived in was so airy and clean. Just opening the door to Graham's room was like walking into some squat in King's Cross, the kind of place I was already familiar with, where the buildings were run down and junkies lived with bare mattresses on the floor and records and trash everywhere. This room did not hold good memories for me. It was strangely quiet without my brother lying on his bed watching television, an ashtray full of fag ends balanced on his chest.

My mother got to work. When she does something, she does it fully and with great determination. I like to think I received that quality from her. We went through everything, each drawer, bookcase, cranny and corner. Everywhere we found the burned foil that my brother had used to "chase the dragon". (This is a method of ingestion in which the user places a substance, usually heroin or crack cocaine, on a piece of foil, lights it from underneath and inhales the smoke.)

My mother started painting and I watched her from the doorway, not helping and not really wanting to any more. But as I watched her face, so intent on what she was doing and so wanting his room to look nice for him, I knew that she truly did love us, no matter what. Why did that realisation not make me feel any better? I thought love was supposed to make you feel whole. My parents loved us both very much, but they didn't understand how we felt. That was what frustrated me.

When Graham left to go for treatment, it was the first time I had been alone. Life felt extremely dull without the drama and it was then that my own addiction began to take hold. It was so easy for me to believe that, just because I wasn't using heroin, I didn't have a problem. I became extremely angry at both my parents and my brother. Suddenly, after everything he had put me through, he was getting all the attention. For a good few years I kept that rage sizzling.

In retrospect, I see now that my brother was the catalyst for me to change and to get the help I needed. In a strange way I am truly grateful, not for his terrible addiction but that he eventually cried out for help. It got my attention and led me ultimately into support groups and into the work I needed to do to heal myself. I was able to stop focusing on him and to eventually demand the respect that I finally realised I deserved. But at the time he went into rehab, I was still far from my own healing. Drugs seemed an incredibly easy solution to my problems. For one thing, they took away the wrenching pain and allowed me to function without feeling constantly depressed and inadequate. They also dissolved my separation anxiety. Suddenly I could stay away overnight whenever I wanted without any repercussions.

I smoked my first joint with my brother just before I turned fifteen. My girlfriend and I were sitting in his room, watching him smoke, and I decided I wanted to try it. My friend was horrified but Graham was amused. He handed me a joint and they both stared as I told them I felt wobbly and strange. I giggled a little but on the inside, I perceived an awakening that I had never experienced before. I felt alive! Perhaps life wasn't going to be so bad after all. Maybe, up until that moment, I just hadn't found the secret to happiness and now here it was! This was the connection that I had been missing. This was the way to fill that terrible void.

Drugs were a godsend. My fears vanished, I could sleep, I felt invincible. I stopped caring what people thought about me. I had confidence. I began to wear sexy clothes and stopped hiding my bottom with big sweaters (for fear it was too large), and men became interested in me. This was a volatile mix – I was still handling being a teenager, with all the emotions that come with puberty, as well as trying to find myself. The fact that I didn't know who I was or where I came from just exacerbated my difficulties. What was wrong with me? After all, I had a family. Wasn't I grateful for that? I was so confused and mixed up and angry and afraid that the only solution was to make a strong commitment to not feel any of it. And so I blundered on with no sense of direction. I never gave any thought about what I wanted to do or achieve, and I failed miserably at school. I could never concentrate or absorb any information that was given to me. If anyone had asked me what year I was studying in history, I couldn't have said. I had a lot of anxiety about failing and spent a great deal of time worrying.

The same year I smoked my first joint, I started smoking cigarettes. Together with my girlfriend I was also snorting solvents. We would spend our time during the library period asking to borrow Tippex thinner fluid from the more studious girls, which we would shake onto our blue sweater sleeves and inhale. The chemicals made our heads spin and we would walk into walls and laugh hysterically. It took a while for the teachers to realise what was going on. We were finally caught after a girl whom we had been threatening if she didn't give us her solvent told the headmistress.

We were summoned to the head's office. I remember standing before the huge brown wooden desk, piled with mountains of paperwork that almost hid our headmistress from view. She was short and round and always wore a black cape, like a cartoon superheroine. Sometimes I'd imagine her in danger of being caught in a strong wind and lifted off her tiny pudgy feet. As my girlfriend and I stood sheepishly side by side, waiting for her to speak, I suddenly found her extremely funny looking. Since I was still slightly high from all that solvent sniffing, I started to giggle. My friend, who really could barely stand up straight, wobbled beside me and began to laugh too. The headmistress seemed a little unsure of what to do and I was sure I could see her trying to suppress a smile. Finally, she spoke in a loud commanding voice. If we had any brain cells to begin with, she told us, we would surely lose them if we continued our current behaviour. If we did not cease immediately, a letter would be sent to our parents. We managed a feeble apology and left the room, still giggling. We went off to find a place to hide where we could have a cigarette and tell the other girls what had happened.

Moving on to college didn't change my habits: I smoked dope, snorted substances and spent my time arranging weekends and finding unsuitable men to fall in love with. I ended up taking a course in child development, as my mother felt it was important for me to have something to 'fall back on'. I was too scared not to follow her advice.

Addiction, I have come to learn, can take many forms. Before I went to any recovery programmes, I truly believed that to be an alcoholic or a drug addict you needed to lose everything you owned and be sleeping under Waterloo Bridge. In fact, it is how those substances make you feel when you are using them and why you choose to do it that determine whether or not you are an addict, and the good news is that you don't have to reach rock bottom before you decide to stop. In my own case, using drugs, food and cigarettes only created more fear and more pain. Finally, they had such an extreme debilitating effect on me that I couldn't get on with my life with them or without them.

And then, of course, there was the opposite sex, which gave me even more reason to feel depressed and take drugs. From the very beginning of dating, I could never be in a committed relationship. I began a pattern of going for men who were either so available that they scared me, or completely unavailable in one way or another. That made it easy for me to see them as the problem and not myself. But usually, when the relationship was over, I would feel devastated. The feelings of separation were so powerful that I often wondered, 'Why is this so intense? I really wasn't that interested, and now I feel as if I can't be away from him.'

I could write endless stories of all the drugs I took, the parties I went to, the blackouts and all the so-called relationships, but I would rather tell you about what lay underneath it all. No matter how many drugs I did or how many boyfriends I had, the moments of freedom from depression and fear were fleeting and, as time went on, the drugs barely covered my feelings at all. I so wanted to be accepted by people and had a terrible fear of rejection, yet I set myself up over and over again by befriending people who would reject me or make fun of me, by choosing boyfriends who already had girlfriends or wives. Ultimately there was never any real union or commitment. Smoking cigarettes and sniffing solvents helped. I acted tough, was outspoken and behaved wildly, traits for which I became infamous. The other girls laughed and I got attention, yet I never revealed to anyone how bad I felt inside.

I spent so much time living in my head, thinking, trying to figure everything out. I tried to control everything – how to get the drugs, how to get the man, how to make my friends keep on liking me. At the end of a day, I'd be so exhausted that my inner fear often escalated to sheer panic. Trying to hide it all from others became harder and harder, and I didn't know how to tell anybody the truth. I had no anchor, nothing solid to hold on to.

As soon as college was over, I took a job as a waitress, which enabled me to maintain a lifestyle with little structure. Drugs and alcohol were forever available, and I became submerged in the nightlife, off to clubs after work to keep the party going and falling into bed at some early morning hour. Something had changed in me at this time. I had crossed some invisible line. I wasn't bothered by what people thought of my behaviour and I began to act inappropriately most of the time. I had no care for rules and regulations. I often stole from work, acquiring all the things we needed for our kitchen, the cutlery, the plates, mugs . . . My flatmate would request more teaspoons and I wouldn't think anything of it. One day I reversed my mother's car up to the back door of the kitchen and put in her boot a large chocolate fudge cake, whipped cream, utensils and a couple of bottles of wine. I always felt justified. When the chemist across the street from where I stole most of my make-up began to suspect me I simply changed shops.

I remember the manager of the restaurant calling me into his office. 'Zara, I am concerned about . . .'

'Really? What?' I was genuinely surprised.

'You take a lot of drugs and I am worried for you.'

I was overcome with surprise and thanked him for his concern but not to worry, I was really fine. I walked away thinking how sweet he was to have thought about me.

When I ran out of the drugs I needed, mainly "grass", I would take it upon myself to find a dealer, usually in any pub that I saw along the way. I was proud of my so-called gift and took friends from time to time to watch me while I walked in, had a good look around and seemed to sniff the dealers out. I would boldly approach a group and ask them if they had anything to sell and ninety-nine per cent of the time I came out with the drugs I wanted. I would also find men at parties whom I felt were easy to take advantage of. I'd lead them on and then find a way to escape before anything physical could happen. I was extremely manipulative once I realised that I had some power and yet still suffered from chronically low self-esteem. It was a cruel mix.

Occasionally, I used to show up at twelve-step support meetings for families with addicts but ended up meeting a man a good sixteen years older than myself who gave me cocaine and listened to me moaning about my family, not understanding me. I thought he was great. It was only when he began to charge me for the cocaine I was using that I got fed up with him. After all, I didn't have the money to pay for it! I had no idea that this man was an addict and dealer too, well into his own denial. This was a very dark period of my life and it took me a few years to totally get away from him.

During this time, I used to visit my brother in rehab on the weekends. In some ways, I felt quite jealous of him: he had new friends, was staying in a beautiful home and seemed happier, in some ways, than I had ever seen him. On one occasion I showed up and his hair had been braided with colourful beads like Stevie Wonder. How much recovery was he doing? It looked like one big party to me.

Graham told me one day that a guy he was in treatment with thought I was cute and wanted to go out with me. I was immediately curious and once I saw Mark, agreed that on his day off we could go out together. I took Mark over to my friend's house and smoked a joint in front of him and danced around the bedroom while he just sat on the floor watching us. We went out a couple more times when he came out of treatment, but eventually I got a phone call from him saying he wasn't allowed to see me any more as his counsellor didn't think I was good for his recovery. After that I used to call him from parties but I would just listen to him talk and then put the phone down.

This was the Eighties. Madonna was hitting the charts and I admired her attitude. I once heard her being interviewed; she stated that as a young child she had lost her mother, and I became riveted to the TV set as she talked openly about her loss. As I listened, I felt a stirring inside and empathy for Madonna. I never mentioned it to my friends. After all, they didn't see me as a child who had lost her mother.

I began to dress a little punky. I hankered after the lacy tights that seemed to be everywhere since Madonna had arrived; I went to the hip girls' shop and put on a pair in the changing rooms. Then I pulled my black leggings over the top, leaving space to reveal the lace from my calf down to the tops of my pointy boots, just as I had seen her do. 'I must have them,' I thought. I looked so cool! The need was incredibly strong, but the tights were expensive. I didn't have that kind of money, so I rolled down my leggings to cover them and walked out of the shop. I was thrilled as I realised I was going to get away with it.

7
Rock 'n' roll lifestyle

It was right after my daughter was born that I started having therapy. I began to have nightmares of self-destruction –
I was the only one alive. I joined ALMA [Adoptees Liberty Movement Association] and felt for the first time that I wasn't the only adoptee in the world. Veronica

When I was twenty, I decided to join a band. My girlfriend told me that one night, at a friend's gig a few years earlier, I had stood stoned at the front of the stage and declared to her, 'You see those guys on stage? That's going to me soon.' I had no recollection of having said that, but it was something to do at the time and my current boyfriend was encouraging. He was also part of the band and suggested we could do backing vocals together. One evening, he brought a tape machine over to my flat and we sat in the living room where he clapped me on and recorded my voice over a song to pretend that I had done the original backing vocals. The idea was to make it look as if I had some experience; in reality, all I had ever done was dance and sing alone in front of the mirror or with my girlfriends in their bedrooms while we drank and smoked lots of dope.

I went for the audition and got the job. It was easy to see why: the lead singer took a fancy to me. It was fun. It was something I had loved ever since my childhood days of writing out lyrics and singing every part. I loved music and the emotional release it provided. Unfortunately, after I joined the band, other things got in the way and everything got a bit messy. I left the backing vocalist and took up with the lead singer. My former boyfriend was extremely upset and quit the band. A girl called Sonny soon joined to replace him and we became good friends. We did our first gig together at Camden Palais with the band Party Hula. It was 1984 and Sonny was working as a backing vocalist with several established musicians, including Bob Geldof on his new album *Deep in the Heart of Nowhere*. Her boyfriend at the time was a brother of the singer Nick Kamen whose career was beginning to take off. I was in awe of her: she was an incredible singer and beautiful and she took me under her wing. She seemed to think I needed mothering! I was growing tired of waitressing and hearing her talk about her career made me realise that I wanted to make more of my life.

About four months after I started with Party Hula, I was at Sonny's house when a record company happened to call to ask if she knew another girl who would be available to be on a video and TV show for Geldof. Yes, she said, there was just such a girl at her house right now. I couldn't believe it when she got off the phone. I had been in a few videos but never considered myself to be at the stage she was at.

As soon as she put the phone down she started organising me. We looked at clothes and she brushed my hair and made up my face. We both knew the record company man wanted to see what I looked like and the whole charade was funny but also extremely embarrassing to me. The doorbell rang and in he came, obviously embarrassed himself, as Sonny started talking and touching my face. 'Well, what do you think? Isn't she cute and she has great teeth!' She thought this was hilarious but, by this point, I just wanted to be swallowed up into the ground. The record company man could barely look at me but managed to mutter, 'Oh yes, she's fine. Great. Very nice.' He brought out various contracts he wanted me to sign for TV shows and the video and told me that, if they couldn't get hold of the other established backing vocalist they wanted, the gig would be mine. He would recommend me to the band and I would know the answer the next day. I couldn't quite take in what was happening.

The next morning, Sonny woke me with a cup of tea, singing, 'Zar got the job! Zar got the job!' I was ecstatic. I couldn't believe my luck. I had done only one gig in my life and that week I was about to appear with Geldof and his band on the *Terry Wogan* talk show, as well as performing in the video for the single. There were plans for other dates as well.

I met Bob for the first time on the day of filming for his video. He was really friendly but I couldn't think of anything to say, so pretended that I was slightly bored by the whole thing. I was extremely nervous, not just because of meeting Bob but also about being surrounded by all the people involved. I really had hardly any experience and was convinced they would somehow find out. The one thing I did have going for me was that I loved being in front of a camera. It never fazed me. By the end of the day I was more relaxed and chatty and enjoyed the attention I received as the new girl in the group.

So began my introduction into the heart of the music industry. With Sonny as my partner, I began to do all the music TV shows around Europe. We worked not only for Bob but also for Matt Bianco and Nick Kamen and any other bands who wanted us, either individually or together. We appeared on *Top of the Pops*, *Saturday Night Live*, *Wogan* and *The Old Grey Whistle Test*, as well as zooming over to Paris, Germany, Spain, Italy, wherever we were needed to mime on a music show. It was so much fun and so easy. It seemed ridiculous to me that we would get paid for miming on TV, staying in a fancy hotel, driving in a limo and eating and drinking basically whatever we wanted. It felt great to just pack up and escape from my mundane life, to live in a nice hotel surrounded by people who paid me attention simply for being 'one of the band', to have my hair and make-up done before I went on stage to help promote the band's latest single.

I began to watch intently how people behaved. How did the other girls in the bands act? How did they walk, talk, dress? I tried to imitate them, adding more swing to my hips and more make-up to my face. For a time I felt great. All the attention was intoxicating, but it never took away the deep void that seemed to be my constant companion.

After a few months, Bob wanted to go out on the road and do a live tour with the band, but Sonny had different plans and she left. We ended up hiring a new girl, Melanie, who was outgoing and confident but new to this world. We became close friends, confiding in each other our insecurities and plans to get back at the band, who enjoyed how naive we were. One day, at rehearsal, they told us to bring the outfits we were going to wear on stage because we were having a dress rehearsal. Melanie and I dutifully went off to change our clothes and when we came back the band fell about laughing. They hadn't changed. They had just wanted to see us in our short skirts.

Bob didn't want us to dress up too much. He would have been fine if we just wore jeans and shirts but Melanie and I were determined to add some style and sexiness to our outfits. We made sure we got our way except one time when we both came out wearing black leotards and fishnet tights; Bob looked us up and down in shock and said, 'No, no way! You look like fricking trapeze artists!'

Our tour was mainly around Italy but we also visited Denmark, Sweden and Germany. Of course, I packed far too many things, not realising I wouldn't get any sympathy or help with my bags. Our tour manager, "The Mick", came from Birmingham and had such a strong accent that it could be hard to work out what he was saying. 'Come on boilers,' he'd yell as Melanie and I struggled behind the rest of them with our bags. 'It's your fault. I told you I wouldn't carry your stuff. Jesus, what have you got in there, your bleeding kitchen sink?'

Mick had a huge belly with a thick scar that ran down the middle. He loved to show it to us and regale us with horror stories of the fights and injuries he had sustained, but I still don't know the tale behind that particular wound.

I can't remember when I told the band that I was adopted but as soon as they knew, The Mick would sidle up to me and whisper in my ear, 'I met your mother on a Beatles tour. . .' I would look horrified, my head spinning. Was there any chance Mick could be related to me? He seemed to take great pleasure from my discomfort and yells of 'Ooh yuck!' and, even though he couldn't possibly be my father, I found myself analysing his face.

I was pretty naive in many ways, despite having recently been hanging out in squats in London's King's Cross with friends who were junkies. In particular, I had a boyfriend whom I adored and often stayed with in "the buildings". They were structurally unsafe and ready for demolition any day, but somehow I thought it was all quite romantic. I'd take the tube from my parents' lovely neighbourhood to the notorious area where pimps and prostitutes lurked at night, and I'd walk the long streets to my boyfriend's house, high as a kite and unafraid as men slowed their cars and asked, 'How much?' I would raise my fingers to them and strut off, happy because I was going to get my boyfriend fix. He made me feel OK about myself, even if it was for just one evening.

But my life had begun to take a new turn. The musicians I was now working with were making something of their lives; they were successful and eventually I managed to get away from all the heroin addicts. I wanted more for myself, but my new milieu became just another avenue for me to keep running away from my problems. Drugs and alcohol were even more available and worse: it was acceptable to have dinner with a drink, to perform with a drink and possibly other substances to keep you going. After all, partying all night was tiring.

We travelled regularly around Europe and got to see many beautiful places. I got a little confused by this new lifestyle and once spent the whole day thinking that we were in Sweden when actually we were in Denmark, much to the amusement of the band. On another occasion, we were sitting in an airport lounge when our tour manager gave us some money in an envelope and told us to exchange it as we were on our way to the next country. I took the envelope and went up to the exchange counter. I told the lady what I needed and waited as she took out my money. She began to study the notes, holding them in the air to look at, which I thought was normal. Then she started talking to me in broken English and looked quite flustered. She said there was a problem with the money. 'Oh no,' I assured her, 'the money is fine. I just need it exchanged.' She became a little stern. 'Please wait.' She picked up the phone and spoke quickly and looked at me. 'This money is fake.' I turned around to see all the band sitting on the sofa laughing and laughing. They had set me up! My tour manager had somehow found this fake money for another joke and I had fallen for it yet again.

Gigs were fun but often unpredictable. One night in Greece the stage was in the middle of a huge soccer field and the crowd was behind on the bleachers. We could barely see them. The company said we couldn't have them near the stage for safety reasons but Bob thought it was ridiculous and yelled at them to come forward. The delighted crowd raced dancing to the front of the stage. As we were singing, a guy standing at the very front, his head level with the stage, started heckling Melanie and me. 'You English whores!' he'd yell in between songs, 'You English tarts.' We glanced at each other and kept singing, making the V sign at him with our fingers and he carried on. By this time, Bob had noticed what was going on and in the middle of a song, with no hesitation, guitar in hand, he went over and kicked the guy in the head. Blood came spurting out of his nose and a huge fight broke out at the front of the stage. The band kept playing, Melanie and I looking at each other, not really sure what to do. As the song finished, the security called us off stage and said we had to leave but the changing rooms were way over on the other side of the field. The crowd was getting angrier and Simon, who looked after Mel and me, took our hands and said we had to run across to the distant building. We hoped the crowd wouldn't notice us but they did. Half way across the pitch I turned to see a huge swarm of people running towards us. I began to scream, 'I can't run, my shoes, my shoe . . .' We both had high heels on and Simon literally dragged us along, shouting, 'Don't stop' until we made it into the building before the crowd descended.

The tour rolled on and I carried on falling in love with unavailable men. I was fascinated by the way some of the men I met could be so detached about love and sex. Most of them had wives or girlfriends at home, but it didn't seem to bother them at all. It was just normal to have flings and then go home and be finished with it until the next part of the tour. I tried to behave like them to show that I, too, really didn't care that much. I had my share of passionate nights and the next day I would be cool and offhand. When we went to night clubs I'd pretend to be interested in other men, when really it wasn't what I wanted at all. I drank more to push it all away.

I continued to love singing and performing but, as the months passed, I couldn't relax. My anxiety seemed to come back in full force when I was alone and after each gig I wondered if it would be my last. I was OK when I was surrounded by people and parties and performing, but every time I came home from a trip, a yawning emptiness threatened to engulf me, an emptiness that grew bigger when I was alone in the quietness of my home. The stillness began to bring me to my knees. I simply couldn't deal with my feelings any more. I couldn't keep up with my lifestyle and the pressure I felt to look good, to stay thin, to be continually beautiful and in control. I was completely devoid of self-esteem.

I felt so insane, so full of fear and rage, that I found even the simplest of tasks stressful. Of course, I had always had feelings of rage that would come out in all the wrong places. Afterwards, I felt extreme guilt, shame and self-hatred. I had no control.

I had no idea how to change the way I was feeling except by using drugs and men, but these didn't seem to be working any more. Some days, driving in my usual risky way, I contemplated aiming my car into a wall. I'd speed up, dodging cars, slamming on my brakes and sticking my finger out of the window and swearing at whoever I thought was in my way. If I thought I was right (which was usually the case), I would get out of my car and approach the motorist, who would either swear back or roll up the window quickly for fear of what I might do. My anger grew so big that I didn't care what happened to me – I just knew that I wanted relief.

I have heard many people say that it wasn't a big crisis in their lives that led to change, just one small thing that made them recognise they had had enough. It was the same for me. I could deal with hanging out with drug users in a dangerous part of London when I was seventeen, my brother being put in treatment when I was nineteen, my mother undergoing heart surgery when I was twenty-one. What I couldn't manage was regular day-to-day life.

The end of my drug use wasn't all that dramatic. Physically I wasn't suffering too much – just short of breath from all those cigarettes. I hadn't lost a home, job, money, husband or children as many other people do. But one day all the drugs, the parties, the lure of the spotlight stopped working for me. I knew that none of those things would make me feel better about myself. I remember sitting with a man whom I had met a few years before when my brother was in treatment and who had became like a mentor for me. I believed then that I didn't really have a problem, the problem lay with my brother and my parents. They just didn't understand me; they needed to sort themselves out and the sooner they did, the better it would be for me. This kind man seemed to take an interest and listened to me open up slowly about my feelings. He appeared non-judgemental and was available to me every week.

Over three years, he spoke to me gently, saying very little as I disappeared for weeks on end, drinking and drugging. I always came back with new stories of boyfriends who were too old or too married – until one evening, at the end of August 1987. I was telling him my usual stories of woe, when he suddenly looked at me directly and said, 'Zara, you are twenty-two years old and you are killing yourself.'

I felt like someone had kicked me in the solar plexus. I knew at that moment without a shadow of a doubt that he was right, and the truth was that I couldn't stop on my own. I stared back at him, unable to speak. I always find that moment strange, because this man had told me the same thing many times before. But until that night, I simply wasn't ready to hear him. I left his office trembling. I knew something needed to change – and quickly.

I walked along the wet dark street and past a late-night newsagent. The pull to go inside took me over, but I didn't buy alcohol. Instead I bought chocolate, a few packets of various favourites, and started to rip open the packet before I was even out of the shop. Inside my head, a voice told me, 'Zara, it's over. You've got to stop.' 'I can't stop, but I don't want to die,' I replied to myself.

I made it into my friend's apartment where I was renting a room. She wasn't at home and I was glad. I found my stash of dope and rolled a joint, telling myself to stop, but my hands had a will of their own. Fear seized me. I knew my life wasn't working, I knew in that moment I was in such trouble that if I carried on in the same way, I wouldn't make it to old age.

I had been attending some twelve-step meetings, as was suggested at the time my brother entered treatment. Those meetings were for people with addicts in the family; they were helpful for encouraging me to be able to talk about my brother, but I still wasn't focused on myself. It wasn't until they realised that I was high in those meetings that people gently suggested I needed to go to another programme for help with drugs and alcohol. I was still in a lot of denial and wasn't sober when I attended those meetings either. I was always shocked by how other participants knew, but they befriended me without judgement and I always remember what they said: 'Get on your knees and ask for help. No matter what you believe, just take the action.' I had thought it silly and embarrassing at the time. I also wasn't sure what I believed in but what did I have to lose? Desperation overcame the fear of how I would look, and weeping, I got on my knees and prayed to God – or whoever was out there – in a way I had never done before.

Afterwards, I lay down on my bed and felt an incredible presence that filled me with strength, a calmness that I had never experienced, a feeling that all was going to be OK, that I was safe, that I was cared for. Even though my face was pressed against the sheets, the darkness of the room lightened. I turned my head till I was looking up at my curtainless window. The light was white and bright, but I couldn't work out where it was coming from. It seemed to stream straight through the glass from the night sky onto my bed. 'You're stoned, Zara,' I told myself, and without further thought, I fell asleep.

8
Turning points

When I had my daughter I started to wonder where I had been in my first three months of life and who had taken care of me. I had been adopted at three months and could see how attached I was to my daughter and how attached she was to me. I thought, how could my mother have done that? Doreen

When I woke up the next morning, the desire for drugs and alcohol was gone. Instead, I was suffused with the strongest desire to change my life and a willingness to take whatever steps were necessary to effect that change. I'm not saying I didn't feel shaky that day but I felt a strength within myself that I hadn't experienced before. I had made the decision that I wanted to change and suddenly felt hope, a glimmer that I *could* feel different. I also knew that I couldn't keep going the way I was. From that day to this, I have never touched drugs or alcohol, even when I have wanted to.

When I began my sobriety, many friends said to me that I really didn't have a problem, yet others recognised that I did. The truth of the matter is that my body probably could have taken more, but my mind and soul couldn't. The depression and pain were so severe that killing myself had begun to look like a reasonable option. Regardless of anyone else's opinion, they weren't living inside my head. I had reached a point where I had to make a choice: Did I want to live? Or did I want to die? And while I was waiting to die, did I want to live a miserable, fearful existence full of extreme anxiety, confusion, and anger, involved with people who didn't have my best interests at heart?

The change after that night when I had finally had enough was indeed miraculous. I began to attend twelve-step programmes and held on to them like a shipwrecked woman to a life raft. Now, though, came the scary part: to walk into a roomful of people and listen to their stories was one thing, but to open my mouth and reveal what was inside me was terrifying. Nevertheless, once I did, I felt tremendous relief and more. It also pushed me to look my demons squarely in the eye, to start taking responsibility for myself and to not give up on this new chance of life.

I had such a wonderful high at the beginning of my sobriety – nothing to do with chemicals. I had an inner certainty that at last I was doing the right thing. That, finally, I could find relief from all the depression and pain, I truly could live another way, and I was thrilled. I remember zipping around in my little blue mini and shouting at the top of my voice my gratitude to God, the universe, a higher power . . . I didn't really mind whom I talked to. I wasn't especially religious – I still wasn't sure if there was a God or not. All I knew was that something was working. It could just have been the inspiration of so many people staying sober together. I would meet up with all my new friends and they would laugh with delight. I was truly buzzing with a feeling that, no matter what anyone said, I had something I had never before experienced – peace of mind – and I was going to hang onto it tightly.

I was sober for just a few weeks when I was invited out bowling on a Saturday night by a group of fellow recoverees. I was horrified. 'Bowling!' I exclaimed. 'You go *bowling* on a

Saturday night?' I felt terribly depressed. Was this what my life had come to? What about all the parties and the gigs? Nevertheless, I decided to go. My new friends laughed at me kindly as I complained that my life was finally over. But I was so drawn to them. They had laughter in their eyes and a brightness that I had never seen before. They were actually enjoying their lives, able to appreciate the simple things, and they weren't drinking or taking drugs.

So off we went to the bowling alley and – surprise! –I *loved* it. I got the knack of it quickly and suddenly became extremely competitive. It was fun and it felt real. I talked with strangers about life and feelings in a way I had never done before. At first, I wasn't ready to reveal too much, so I mainly listened. Then, as time passed, I began to slowly let them see some of my tears. Showing my vulnerability was the hardest part and still is. Yet, paradoxically, it is the sharing of that vulnerability that leads to greater strength and acceptance; it is always healing.

As I began my recovery around these issues, I slowly began to see that I had been reliving over and over that first rejection by my birth mother, playing it out in different ways instead of grieving the original loss. Adopted people are rarely told, 'You need to grieve, because it is a death to not know your mother. You cannot replace her with a new one.' But society is only barely beginning to recognise this, and for most of us, the grieving has to be done alone and hidden from others. I had carried that grief since birth and only now did I begin to get glimpses of what lay beneath my anger. I wasn't such a tough nut after all. I began to see that, yes, I did have feelings about being adopted. I wanted to know the truth. I needed my story. Living in the shadows was too hard. How could I go forward with no beginning? How could I feel connected to anyone when I didn't even know where I came from? The jokes I had always made about myself, saying I was a mistake because I was probably the result of a one-night stand, were a cover-up for the fear that my mother had been raped, that I was the product of an act of violence.

It became clear very early in my sobriety that a lot of changes had to be made. I wasn't going to get well overnight – that much was apparent. If I had known when I walked into my first meeting how much stuff I had to look at and how long it would take, I would probably have run screaming straight out of the door.

Those first five years showed me how much work needed to be done. My family knew I was attending meetings. It had been suggested when my brother went into treatment that we all seek some group counselling, but my parents didn't feel it was for them. Now, they would just ask me if I were going to a meeting. It wasn't a secret, yet like adoption, it was never discussed.

Unfortunately, not all my friends could be happy for me and I knew that staying sober depended on letting go of my old life. This was a terrifying realisation: if I gave up those friends, that lifestyle, who would I be? For the first year, I carried on my same pattern of dating unavailable men. But now it was much harder because I had nothing to anaesthetise those awful feelings. I travelled occasionally with the bands I used to work with: I went to Australia and New Zealand with Geldof and on a support tour for the girls' band Bananarama with Perfect Day, but I found it all very hard. Being back in the cocoon of touring on a bus, staying sober, watching other people act out, part of me wanting to dive straight in there with them, I began to see that there were certain jobs I just wasn't ready for, especially being away from home for so long. It wasn't easy. I felt pretty confused about my career as that's where my identity had been forged. I tried desperately to pretend that I could handle them, but it didn't work. I felt frustrated and angry. Letting go of my old life was feeling too hard and drugs began to look appealing. This time, though, I knew they would kill me. I didn't want to go down that road.

I had to give it all up – the boyfriends, the deceit – and live on my own. I had to accept that maybe some women could sleep with married men or date men who weren't interested in a committed relationship, but I, Zara, could not. I *always* got emotionally involved and it felt terrifying. But by now it was obvious that no one could make me whole, no one could fix me but *me*.

I was angry as hell. What, no relationships? No men to tell me I was OK, to lust after me? How could I cope without those affirmations? Who would I be? My identity came from the clothes I wore, the bands I was in, the men who pursued me. 'It is too hard to do this!' I yelled at my sober friends.

'Just give yourself some time out to get to know yourself. We promise it won't kill you.' I knew they were right. It was too hard to live the way I was, stuck, trapped, dependent on outside sources for any sense of self-worth. A tiny voice within me said, 'You have to try. It will be worth the effort.'

When I was sober for about a year, I realised that it was time to start dressing differently. I had always dressed in revealing clothes that got me the attention I craved, but that would have to change. Who would I be without this mask? I decided to do an experiment. I packed up all my clothes – the red velvet backless number, the leather miniskirt, the skin-tight red dress with all those hooks up the back. Come to think of it, there were a lot of red garments and a lot of black. They had to go. After all, if the new me was about to reveal herself, I couldn't be wearing old-me clothes.

I remember vividly saying to myself a few years earlier, as I stood in my fishnets, black velvet miniskirt and my favourite backless top, wearing bright red lipstick and with a long cigarette dangling out of my mouth, 'I just want men to like me for *me*!' Well, if they could have seen past the face paint, they might have. But in reality, all the paraphernalia of so-called fashion was a shield to keep everyone away. Genuine intimacy had never entered my life.

Finally, all the clothes were tied up in bags in my flat. They had been there for a few days, when my friend Carol came to visit. I announced that I'd decided to sneak a few items back 'just in case'. 'Just in case *what*?' Carol exclaimed. I was caught. I knew I had to be willing to change, to take the risk of not hiding anymore. I began to see how much I needed those clothes and that was pretty scary. After all, they were only clothes!

I began to choose a different wardrobe, less revealing and more conservative, yet still smart and stylish. These were things that I had never looked at in the past for fear that they weren't eye-catching enough. But as I began to find balance, I started to feel quite comfortable. I also stopped wearing make-up for a while. One evening I arrived at my parents' house for dinner with relatives and my mother, not knowing what was going on, asked me if I wanted to borrow her make-up, as she could see I wasn't ready!

Actually, once I stopped looking out the corner of my eye to see if the workmen would still whistle at me if I wore baggy clothes, I started to let go. The focus of my life began to change; it mattered less what people thought. It was as though I had stepped off the merry-go-round, and it was extremely liberating. I could now observe and realise that for me, the fast life didn't work; it brought only anxiety and despair. I began to experience a freedom that I had never known before and a high on life that no drug had ever induced.

I carried on singing and performing, but this time as a lead singer in bands with people also in recovery or people who were moving in the same direction as I was. I began to write and write – songs of either hope and white light or the pain and anguish of reunion. Although some of these songs were definitely not my best work, they helped channel the emotions without resorting to my usual escape of drugs, cigarettes and a new man. I earned money by cleaning or babysitting. I was always broke, yet I was happier than I had been when money was easy.

I irritated many people by talking about my new lifestyle. After all, it really wasn't for everyone and I had, as usual, gone to the extreme. I still lacked balance. I actually didn't know how to do anything in moderation and many people stayed away as I preached and pranced in my new baggy clothes, celebrating a celibate life. But I felt so much hope. I knew I was more than just my clothes. I knew that relationships didn't have to be all bad and painful. I began to work harder on my relationships with girlfriends and some wonderful friendships developed. Life began to roll along and I started to feel somewhat cured of the old me. I could function without drugs and I could live without a relationship. In fact, I became pretty independent and overconfident, until one day, across a crowded room, I saw an extremely handsome man. Thus began my rapid descent from my high pedestal.

Since becoming sober I had been briefly involved with one man. Fortunately, I was able to see that a relationship with him would bring only pain, and I managed to extricate myself. But for some reason, I couldn't see the danger with this new man. Maybe I felt a desperation that I really would end up alone, perhaps I forgot to trust myself. Nevertheless, it was a painful lesson. He did not want to marry me, he did not want commitment, yet why couldn't I leave? All this recovery and here I was again.

All the feelings of abandonment came crashing back, except this time they were even more intense. Poor bloke, he understood there was something deep going on with me, but how could he really know? He decided to leave London and go back home to New York. The weeks before his departure were one of the most painful times of my life.

I suffered terrible anxiety and kept crying. I began to feel absolutely insane, yet I couldn't walk away. I was staying to the bitter end. I also felt deep shame that anyone should see me so out of control. Even then, it began to dawn on me that the intensity of my grief didn't quite match the situation.

After he had gone, I had a very difficult time. Deep loneliness and grief were, it seemed, continually with me. Some mornings, I would wake up in a panic, wondering how I was going to make it through the day, and I'd call friends to calm me down. One night, as I lay down to go to sleep, I found myself crying from a deep place. I cried about every relationship I had ever been in. I cried because I had never taken care of myself, and I began to feel sorry for what I had done to *me*. I had treated myself so badly!

That night proved to be another turning point. When I awoke the next day, I made a pact with myself: I would never hurt myself in that way again. I would be a friend to myself, and if I couldn't have a marriage based on real union, I would rather be alone. Anything less just wasn't worth the pain. I tearfully called a girlfriend, Gina, and said, 'Well, it looks like I will never get married and have children if I stay on this path. After all, I don't seem very exciting.'

I look back on that experience and realise that each time I got involved in those situations, I felt extreme pain at the thought of separation. At the time, I never understood that any separation triggered the initial loss of my birth mother.

9
The search

I am glad that I searched, since there was some serious medical history. I am resentful that the sealed record system prevented me from getting to know my birth mother. Dinah

I needed to know who my birth mother was. This fact surfaced quite early in my recovery. I confided this to the man who had been helping me a lot at that time. His response was so simple. 'Why don't you?' he replied. I was shocked. 'What do you mean, why don't I?' I said, 'Because I am not allowed.' Surprised, he pointed out that I was an adult and that, in England, the records were open. I just had to take it one step at a time.

It appeared that all I had needed was a green light, someone to tell me it was OK. I threw myself into the search. It generated so much anxiety that the only way I could get through it was to tell myself, 'Zara, you don't have to meet her. Just gather the information.' At that time, I earned an irregular living that gave me time to pursue the information gathering. I worked as an extra on a number of TV shows and had walk-on roles in a few films – I had never wanted to be an actress so it suited me perfectly being around studios and fun people without having to be at the centre. I also did TV work with bands and a little touring. But I had to be very careful who I was around, since my sobriety was so new and fragile. That led me to turn down some very attractive offers with bands. I also did babysitting, cleaning, auditioning and singing in a band with other people in recovery. Sometimes I claimed unemployment. Most of the time I was pretty broke, but I had so much heavy emotional work to do that not being too busy was a bonus.

Too afraid they would be angry, hurt, and would reject me, I never told my adoptive parents what I was doing. I needed the time to do my research alone and absorb each piece. I sent off for my information and was told I needed to see a social worker, who would assess whether I was mentally stable enough. Of course, they didn't quite say that, but I read the subtext. When I went to my first meeting with the assigned social worker, I wanted to do my best to come across as a very well-adjusted human being. I didn't want to give anyone an excuse to keep things from me.

At the time, I was living in a bedsit. It was very small and my bed took up most of the room. Somehow there was a fridge, sink and even a shower squeezed inside, and with all my belongings, there was no room for anyone else. Nevertheless, I was relatively happy living there. I needed a place to be alone, especially during "the search", where I could sit and cry if need be or just stare at the wall, which I often did, when absorbing piece after piece of who I was.

The social services building happened to be just up the street from where I lived. I didn't know then that I had been born only a few streets away. Although I could easily have walked, on the day of my appointment I drove my little blue mini, anxious to get there as fast as I could. It was cold, mid-January and the sky was almost as grey as the building. Approaching the steps to the main entrance,

I could barely breathe, so I kept focusing on the door. I was almost floating; nothing felt real. I definitely wasn't in my body at all. I saw myself walking in and talking and yet I wasn't connected.

I had lived my whole life in an adoption fantasy story. I had been able to use it to keep people away from me, to not integrate. Up to a point, I liked the feeling of being different, that I had no ties to anyone, didn't belong to anyone. Now I was going to find out that I was just like everyone else – that I had a mother and a father too.

I cannot begin to tell you how strange it all felt. I noticed how normal everyone seemed and how I felt no sense of connection. It was strangely quiet in the main hall. I walked to the receptionist and came face to face with Sarah, an old school friend and flatmate from my Party Hula days. We had travelled to Israel together, where we had drunk and partied and been thrown off the kibbutz where we were staying. Afterwards, we had hitchhiked around Europe and ended up on a Greek island after selling our Walkmans for the boat ticket. One evening, thinking we had been given speed to help us dance all night long, we wondered why we were suddenly so sleepy that we began to pass out at the bar table. When we showed our Greek friends the package the tablets had come in, they laughed hysterically and told us we had been given sleeping tablets. I wandered back to our campsite, crawled into my sleeping bag and slept for fifteen hours.

Sarah and I both smiled. I hadn't seen her in a few years since we had moved out of the flat we shared.

'I can't believe it!' she exclaimed. 'I knew it had to be you. There could be only one Zara Stanton. I asked the social worker to tell me why you were here, but she wouldn't. You know, confidentiality and all that. Wow, it's so good to see you.' She looked at me expectantly.

'I'm here to find out about my birth mother,' I said, my mood still quite subdued.

'I had a feeling you were,' she replied. Just then, the social worker appeared to show me into her office.

'Good luck," Sarah called. 'Let us know what happens.'

The social worker, Alice Clarkson, was a friendly middle-aged woman with black hair, which I thought must be dyed, and a strong stature. She was very chatty and quite excited by the prospect of helping an adopted person. She had never witnessed anyone following through with locating their birth parents. I was glad she couldn't see what was going on inside me.

We sat in her small white-painted office with a large window overlooking the car park out front. She began to talk about me needing some help and counselling. What I was about to embark on could be very emotional and it was always beneficial to talk about my feelings and expectations.

I immediately began to tell her about the wonderful recovery I was doing and that I had a special person who was helping me. The fact that this man knew little, if anything at all, about adoption didn't bother me at the time and she didn't ask. I convinced her that I had all the help I needed and had been working hard on myself (well, only for a few months, but she didn't need to know that) and that I was ready for the information, thank you very much.

So in her next breath, when I least expected it, she told me my birth mother's name. She had a file and she just said her name. It was that simple to her, but for me, it was the most life-changing piece of information I had ever been given. I sat there, not knowing what to say. I was stunned to think that it was that easy, that for all these years people had had access to my birth mother's name. It was too much for me to take in. I was a jumble of emotions but the main thought that ran through my head was that my birth mother was real, she had a name, she existed. All the self-confidence with which I had walked through the door crumbled as I repeated over and over the name of this woman who was my mother.

Both of us decided that I had received enough information for one meeting and I left as quickly as I could. Holding back my tears (God forbid the social worker should see the real me), I scheduled another appointment and somehow made it home.

During the long wait between applying for my file and receiving it, I had a lot of time on my hands, so I found other things I could do to keep the search moving. I went to Catherine House, where I had been so many years before with my schoolmate Nikki. There you can look at anybody's birth, death and marriage certificates. It's an amazing place, a large building with miles of shelves crammed with files and row upon row of tables where you can spread the files out to look down endless columns of names and dates. I enjoyed going there. The sense of anonymity was so nice; no one bothered me. I also liked it that no one knew what I was doing. I had all these relatives who were just busy with their lives, and here I was tracking them down. I felt like this great detective who was uncovering the secret of life. Well, I was. It was the secret of *my* life.

The amazing thing about the place is that I could order anyone's certificates and no one asked questions. When I found my birth mother's birth listed, I ordered the full version of her birth certificate. This would tell me the place of birth, the address where she had lived at the time, her parents' names and their occupations. I was told it would take three days and they could send it to me or I could come back and collect it. I chose to come back; it felt safer. Those three days felt like three years. When I went back and queued up to collect the certificate, I remember expecting someone to demand to know what I was doing. When I finally got to the counter, they handed it over without interrogation and there it was – all the information, the address where she lived, the names of her parents.

At my next appointment with Alice, I learned that I had been born in Finchley at a mother-and-baby home right around the corner from where I currently lived. My name was Paula Sampson. I was so shocked that I wanted to cry. It never occurred to me that my birth mother would have named me. I had always thought of myself as merely a number. That she had named me meant that she had cared enough to think of a name, and I wondered why she had chosen Paula.

In a peculiar coincidence, when my adoptive mother worked with my father in his office, she called herself Mrs Sampson, because she didn't want the clients to know they were related. As a child, I asked my mother why she chose that name. She explained that Sampson was easy to remember, since it was similar to Stanton. As a child, you accept what you are told, but when I found out that Sampson was my birth mother's name, I felt sick to my stomach. My mother tells me it is a coincidence.

Now I could finally order my real birth certificate. Adopted people's certificates are different: all that is listed are your adopted name, date of birth, and names of adoptive parents. Years later, when I applied for my immigration papers in the US, I was told that this birth certificate wasn't a valid document and I had to show them my first original birth certificate. I have no idea what people do if they don't have that information. It is distressing to be told that your birth certificate is meaningless.

I went straight away to the local records office to order my birth certificate, which again was local to where I was living. I was terrified, but luckily I hadn't yet given up cigarettes and they helped numb my feelings as I chained-smoked my way through the ordeal. A chirpy little woman gave me the necessary paperwork and told me to fill it out; processing would take about fifteen minutes. As she busied herself with her work, I waited for her to ask me questions:

What was I doing? Did I think it was right that I should have this information after all the hard work my adoptive parents had done? How I would break their hearts. How selfish of us adopted people to want to know who our natural parents were. Nevertheless, she didn't say a word to me except when I handed her the filled-out forms. 'Thank you, Miss Sampson,' she said. 'Take a seat.'

I nearly died. No, I wasn't Miss Sampson. I was Miss Stanton. I wanted desperately to explain, but I couldn't speak. I sat down on a hard wooden chair and smoked some more. My head spun. Would my father's name be there? Would I get to know about him too? What would it tell me?

Finally I was called. 'Miss Sampson. Miss Sampson?' I think she said it only twice but I can't be sure. I was still getting used to the new name. I took the paper all folded up and went outside to the street. I took a deep breath and opened the certificate. I scanned everything quickly and then went back over it again slowly. There I was, Paula Sampson. That was me. Then it gave my birth mother's name, but where it said 'Father' all I got was . . . And the same with 'Father's Occupation'. Blank. I felt a pain in my heart, fleeting but sharp. The one thing the certificate did give me was the address of where my birth mother had lived at the time of my birth. Maybe her parents were still there.

I think I drove to that address within a couple of days. Too terrified to go alone, a friend, Kerry, came with me. It was in West London, not too far away, just down one long high road, a road I had driven on endless times. Now I was to find the building in which my birth mother had lived and carried me.

That street has never been the same to me since that day. Years later, I still look down it at that grey two-storey building and remember distinctly how I felt the first time I saw it. Now I tell whoever is with me, 'That is where my birth mother lived when she was first pregnant with me.'

It was easy to find the tall block of flats with a park opposite. I had a strong sense I had been in the park before and the building had an eerie quality. I felt I knew for certain that my birth mother had sat in that park or at least walked through it while she was pregnant. We parked and I began to feel the fear set in. I had no idea if her parents still lived there, but I wanted to find out. It was easy to get inside. There was no intercom, or if there was, the door happened to be open, and there we were on the first floor, standing outside number two, the flat she had lived in, where she had found out she was pregnant, where they kept it a secret. I was trembling. What if someone opened the door? What if they *did* still live there? What was I doing and what in heaven's name was I going to say? There were some letters on the ground and I quickly picked them up to look at the name. It wasn't Sampson; someone else lived there now. I was flooded with two distinct emotions – relief and loss. Where were those people now?

I immediately said to Kerry, 'Let's get the hell out of here!' Once outside, I stood for a brief moment and looked at the park again. Then we jumped in the car and drove off, giggling nervously.

Around this time, I finally received my adoption file. It arrived in a brown envelope that I still have. Alice Clarkson gave me some additional papers she wasn't supposed to and asked me to promise to never tell anyone; her job would be on the line. I went home and read over everything I had been given. It was the most painful, liberating, weird experience of my life. I was reading about a baby – Paula – me.

I read how the mother had met an Italian student at a night club. She was sixteen years old and he was twenty-one. They had known each other only a short while when she became pregnant; he offered marriage but she refused. (I was later to find out that the marriage offer was not true.) The birth had been hard for my mother. I was with her only about a week when she became too sick to care for me. Twelve days later, I was placed in foster care. I have never found out where I was or whom I was with for those twelve days. Eventually, suitable parents were found for me. Materially they were able to provide a good home. The woman was a fine homemaker and the man was a lawyer. They also had a little boy, adopted two-and-a-half years earlier. I thought, isn't it interesting that adoptive parents don't adopt just two boys or two girls? They can create the perfect family with the perfect age difference.

One of the most difficult things I learned was that my adoptive parents were interested in me, but that they had already booked their winter holiday for two weeks. Could they pay the fostering fees and pick me up when they got back? I didn't understand how they could not have dropped everything. Didn't they understand that two weeks to a baby without a regular mum was a lifetime? They finally came to meet me on January 4th, 1965. They took me home for the usual probation period with a view to adopt. At the age of two months, I was with my third mother.

After I had finished reading, I cried all night long. I think I was crying for my whole life. I felt grief from the deepest part of my soul. I also felt very strongly the rage that I had always carried, but this time I knew why I was so angry. A bunch of strangers had planned my future without consulting me. Who the hell were they to know what was best for me and where I should be packed off to? I felt as though my birth mother just wanted to get rid of her little problem and get on with her life while my parents wanted to pretend that I was really their child and that I had had no life before them. I didn't feel chosen or special – just betrayed.

I was deeply saddened to find out that my birth mother hadn't been in love with my father, that it had been just a casual affair. Perhaps that was naive of me, but I was still young. Even though I used to joke, 'I was probably the result of a one night stand,' I hadn't realised how much I had hoped for a different reality. The truth was devastating, and it also confirmed what I had always believed about myself, that I was a mistake.

I spent the next few weeks going back and forth to Catherine House and deciding how to get more information. I remember one day looking through file after file for my birth grandmother's details and realising the name didn't match what I had; it was a slightly different spelling. I stood for a while probably looking confused, when out of the crowd a man approached me and asked if he could help. I told him my situation and he said that he helped adopted people trace their families and was writing a book on the subject. He made some suggestions. I showed him the names that all seemed so similar yet were spelled differently and he asked, 'Which one do you feel is right?'

I read one out and said, 'I am so sure it is this one. I feel there is just a spelling mistake.' 'Trust your intuition,' he advised. 'So much of a search is about that.'

Well, I thought, *that's all very well for you to say, but don't you know who I am? I can't do that! How can I trust that part of myself? It has so often got me into trouble!* But the odd thing was, I did begin to trust that voice. It was so strong that I just knew which way to go, as though my whole being was pulling me. The name I chose proved to be the right one and the stranger just seemed to disappear into the crowd.

By looking through every month of every year that I considered she was of marrying age, I found out that my birth mother had eventually got married. There were columns and columns of names, and hers would have been so easy to miss. The writing was so cramped and small. Finding that piece of information gave me a tremendous feeling of accomplishment and I actually became very impressed with myself. I seriously thought I would make a great detective one day, solving mystery after mystery, but I also realised

I was jumping the gun. I had to solve my own mystery first.

I ordered the marriage certificate, which told me that she had married an Italian man who worked as a chef. They were living in Knightsbridge at the time. Although I knew that he couldn't be my birth father, I couldn't help wondering why she had again chosen an Italian. Marrying outside the faith doesn't usually go down well in Jewish families and I wondered how her parents had felt about it.

I continued to look through each year and discovered that they had had a son. (A daughter had been born within a year of their wedding, but I didn't find this out until later). I ordered the son's birth certificate. I could find no other children after him. He was only about twelve years old at the time, and I thought, *Youngest child, most recent address.* The certificate told me where they had been living at the time of his birth. Once again, it was close to where I lived at the time. That was always the strangest part for me – how close to one another we had all been living. Had we passed one another in the car, sat next to each other on the same bus, shopped at the same stores? I had always wondered if we would instantly recognise one another, if I could have picked her out of a lineup.

Once I had this recent address, I dragged my friend Kerry out with me again. When we arrived on the street in question, I hid, petrified, in the car and sent her off knocking on doors. Kerry's story was that my birth mother had been a schoolmate of her own mother and that she wanted to invite her to a reunion. I had fantasies of people saying, 'We are not fooled by your story! We know it's that bastard brat trying to ruin her mother's life. She was given up once. Doesn't she get it?' There were other scenarios, but they always had the same ending: REJECTED in big red letters.

After a while, Kerry came back to tell me that there had been no answer at the actual address, but that she had knocked on a neighbour's door. The neighbour told her that the family had moved a while ago but that she didn't know where. She suggested Kerry call a certain person who lived down the street, because the two families had been very friendly; they would surely help her. I think she even gave Kerry the telephone number.

Wow, I thought, *some neighbour! The next thing you know she will be telling us all the dirt on number 47 and that Mrs So-and-So at number 56 is definitely shagging the postman.* Kerry managed to get away before that happened, and I thanked God for all the gossipy, nosy people in the world. This anonymous former neighbour was a huge key in helping me find my birth mother.

I think I probably drove Kerry nuts over the next few weeks, but she is much too nice to say so. I would go over to her house and she would dial the number and I would shallow breathe, watching her every move. But there was never any answer and I began to feel despondent. We decided that Kerry should try to call at different times in the day and that I didn't need to be there every time, but that was hard to let go. Then I kept calling Kerry to ask if she had tried to phone that day. My poor friend didn't have time every day, so in the end we decided I should try on my own. What a concept! I had been too scared to speak on the phone in case the former neighbour recognised my voice, in case I sounded exactly *like* her. Talk about paranoia!

So I did call and eventually I had some luck. At last a young girl answered and I told my made-up story. She said, 'Oh yes, I know them,' and she said a girl's name, whom I realised must be my sister, and then my brother's name. For a split second I couldn't speak. *Wow, I have a sister, and wow, she knows them! They exist, they are alive!* I managed to compose myself and tried my best to sound as though I was someone who merely needed some casual information. Then she told me they had moved out of London about a year earlier and my heart sank. Did she know where? No, she didn't, but she was sure her mother would. Her mother would be over at her house on Saturday night for a big party, and I should call to speak to her then.

My head spun in a million directions. What if they had moved to Italy? How would I ever find them then? In one way, it seemed I was so close, yet it also felt hopeless. I was scared of knowing and scared of not knowing. It was a very uncomfortable place.

I immediately went and ordered my sister's birth certificate. Her name was Roberta. My childhood friends, the two sisters who lived across the street from me, were called Katie and Roberta. The three of us had been inseparable. I loved those sisters so much (I still do) and longed to be their sister. They had a special bond that real sisters have, and I knew that, as much as they included me, I could never be part of that unique connection. Now, twenty-four years later, I was to find out that I'd had a sister all along and her name was Roberta too.

The day finally came for me to call the neighbours' house. I was terribly nervous and said a quick prayer before I dialled. I say "quick" because it was so hard to be still even for a moment. A girl answered the phone, her voice battling against the background of party sounds, people talking and music playing. It was the same girl who had answered before. I reminded her who I was and that she had said to call that night. Was her mother there, I enquired, and could I speak with her? She told me to hold on and I heard her shout, 'Mum, there's a girl on the phone.' I couldn't hear anymore, just the phone dropping down and the muffled sound of the continuing party. I felt sick. At last the girl came back to the phone and said very casually, 'Me mum said they moved to Weybridge.'

My heart leaped. 'Weybridge,' I repeated, just to make sure.

'Yeah, she said they opened an Italian restaurant down there.'

I stammered 'Thank you,' and we said goodbye.

She didn't ask me a million questions, she didn't wish me luck, she just gave me the information and was gone. Now if someone had called me wanting to know where someone I knew had moved too, believe me, I would have given them the third degree and tried to find out what the scandal was about before I revealed anything.

So there I was with a crucial missing piece of information. I was tired and freaked out. It was as though I had always known I would find out, yet I was aware that really knowing the truth meant crushing the fantasy I had lived in for so long. Until now, my birth mother could be anybody I wanted her to be, depending on my mood that day. Now I was going to find out the truth and that could mean rejection. She might not want to know me at all. But I also knew if that were the truth, I would handle it somehow. I just had to keep moving forward.

10
Contact

Until I met my brother, I had never seen anyone else who looked like me. Irene

The next day, I went with my friend Virginia to visit her sister, who had had a baby a few months before. We really looked forward to the visit, and not only because of the new baby. The sister lived on a houseboat in west London. The canal was beautiful, so green and calm, and although the houseboat was a little rickety-looking from the outside, the inside was delightful. It was warm and cosy, and it was so much fun to sit in the lounge and look out of the window onto the water. The baby, a little girl, was so appealing. She sat in one of those bouncers going up and down with such a funny expression on her face that soon we were all crying with laughter, which made her squeal and laugh too.

I began to update my friends on my search. I told them that only the night before I had found out where my birth mother had moved to. The sisters looked at me and said almost in unison, 'Weybridge is just over there, the next town from here,' and they pointed across the water. Geography never having been my strong point, I managed to mumble an 'Oh,' then an 'Oh, God!' I looked out suspiciously over the water, as if my birth mother and family might suddenly appear before me.

My friends suggested I call Directory Inquiries right away and get the phone number. 'Do you want business or residential?' enquired the operator. She was just an ordinary woman going about her business of giving out a zillion numbers a day. She would never know the significance of what she was about to tell me.

'Both,' I answered. I wrote down and double-checked the numbers, then hung up quickly. No bolts of lightning came out of the sky, no special music or loud booming voice announced to the world that ZARA STANTON HAS LOCATED HER BIRTH MOTHER.

I looked back at my friends, whose eyes had been riveted on me the whole time. 'Did you get it?' they breathed excitedly. I nodded. 'Dial it,' one of them urged.

For a moment I froze. 'OK,' I said presently, 'but be quiet. I am not going to say anything.' With trembling fingers, I dialled the number. A woman answered whom today I know to have been my birth mother. I let her say 'Hello' a couple of times and then I put the phone down.

I asked my friends for a local phone book and got the addresses of both their home and their restaurant. I am still amazed at the series of coincidences that led me that day: that I was at my friend's houseboat so close to Weybridge, that of course she would have a local phone book. It was all so easy, and during that time I felt carried, like there was some force steering and guiding me. When my old fear of rejection came up, I used all my experiences and so-called coincidences to remind myself that I was meant to complete this search and that no matter what, I would be OK.

I wasn't ready to make contact immediately. I needed time to absorb all that I had found out, and of course I needed to spy. I dragged another girlfriend, Wendy, along since it felt too scary to go alone. I say I dragged my friend, but she was quite willing. My venture seemed to be exciting to other people, and they wanted to be involved. As for myself, I was mainly out of my body. It all felt so unreal and too painful to fully connect with what I was doing.

I made the journey to my birth mother's house a week later with my girlfriend helping with directions. As we turned down her street, I thought my heart would jump out of my mouth. It was a small suburban lane with little space between houses, although they were a good size and had expensive cars in the driveways. Pat's house was almost hidden behind bushes, and we found a good place to park on the opposite side of the street where we had some view of the windows and part of the driveway. I had the same feeling that I'd had on the previous search for her house – that I would be recognised immediately. I slid down in the seat for safety, drinking juice and eating the sandwiches I had made. Wendy found it disconcerting. 'How can you eat at a time like this?' I shrugged my shoulders. 'I'm hungry.'

Sitting upright, she stared at the house. I remember her talking as I munched away, saying things like, 'Oh, how sad, your mother is in that house. I sense she must be sad too.' I wanted to throw up. I just couldn't deal with those thoughts. As I was watching Wendy's reaction to it all, someone walked out of the house. The blood rushed to my head. It was a man, average height and build, with a moustache, in his early forties. He walked to the edge of the driveway and stood for a moment. He noticed our car and for a split second stared directly at us.

At that moment, a group of boys cycled past, and one shouted, 'Orlando!' 'That's your brother!' Wendy exclaimed. It was hard to tell which one he was as they were going quite fast, but my friend got really excited. She was convinced she had spotted him. The boys cycled off and the man went inside. We waited a while longer but saw no one else. As we drove away, I felt so relieved. I think I drove up again a couple more times before I actually made contact. I also managed to find their restaurant. It was closed that day, but I looked through the window.

I felt happy that everything – the house, the restaurant – looked so normal. As an adopted person with no information, I had lived a great deal in fantasy about my true heritage, one moment believing my birth mother was a famous movie star, and the next that she was in prison for murdering her best friend or that she was a hooker living in a squat in King's Cross. That she lived in a normal-looking house with a normal-looking car brought me a huge sense of relief.

Not long after I found out where my birth mother lived, I called Alice Clarkson. We talked about the next stage, contacting her. Should we write? Should we call? We jumbled around ideas, but nothing felt good to me – there were so many *buts*. 'But what if we send her a letter and her husband doesn't know and he opens it and he turns into a raving monster and leaves her?' I would say, or 'What if she reads it at breakfast and chokes on her toast?' or 'What if she really has no memory of even having a baby?' The list went on and on and the social worker tried to be reassuring. Personally, I don't think she had a clue either. She was more excited by the fact that in her whole career I was the first adoptee who wanted to complete the reunion with her help. Maybe the other adoptees had more self-esteem than I did at that point because I just wanted to be told what to do. Actually, I didn't know there was another option, that adopted people and birth families could reunite in any way they chose. I still felt that I wasn't really going to be allowed to do this.

The thought of actually calling made me feel sick, so a letter felt like the safest of all the options. It gave me a little more time to compose myself, and we wrote it in a way that gave my birth mother a chance to deny her past if her husband or family didn't know. I was still into protecting everyone, but it was the only way I could handle it. After several revisions – I felt that every word was important – I finally had the letter in hand.

> *Dear Mrs Giocondi,*
>
> *I am trying on behalf of my client to trace members of a family to whom she believes she may be connected. The name of the family she wishes to trace is Sampson, and they lived in the Ealing area around 1964.*
>
> *If you feel you can help and would like to discuss this further, then contact me either by letter or by telephone at the above number.*
>
> *In all cases where one is trying to trace members of families who have lost touch, it is common to write to people who, in fact, have no connection with the people involved, and if this is so, I am sorry to have troubled you.*
>
> *Yours sincerely,*
> *Mrs Alice Clarkson*
> *Social Worker*

I held onto the letter for a couple of days and went to my recovery groups and cried and cried. Although everyone was kind, no one really knew what to say. The truth was that those groups were not about adopted people and no one had any answers for me. A wonderful thing did happen, though. I heard a young woman share that she had recently met some family. Although she was quite vague, I just knew she was adopted. I grabbed her at the end of the meeting, and she said, yes, she had just been reunited with both her birth parents. They were married to one another, and she had three full-blood sisters. We talked a lot, and during the next few weeks she stayed in contact. We became close friends and still are. We continue to talk about the impact of adoption. I am truly grateful she is in my life.

I knew I had to post the letter eventually, but I was so scared. Actually mailing it meant there would be no turning back, that I would really know the truth. The fear of rejection was so strong, but finally the not knowing became unbearable. I dropped the letter into a letter box. Immediately I was engulfed in a wave of panic and dashed off to meet with some friends. 'I want the letter back! What have I done?' I fantasised about running to the letter box and clinging to it for the rest of the night until the postman came so that I could take it back. Yet I knew I had to face this stuff sooner or later, and the truth was I would never really feel like it.

For the next few days, I drifted in a limbo state. I was very jumpy, I couldn't focus on anything, and, looking back, I really don't know what I did to get through the wait. The days felt endless, and every time I went back to my bedsit, I would unlock the door with trepidation and go to the answerphone to see if there was any news. My adoptee friend often called to check in with me. It was a relief to talk to someone who understood.

During all this time, I never told my parents what I was doing. I wasn't ready, so it felt very strange when they called to see how I was, to say that all was OK and keep everything back. I was too scared that my mother would be hurt. I knew that I needed to focus on myself and couldn't risk taking on my mother's feelings, something I always did in those days. I was also a very immature twenty-four-year-old who was as terrified of my adoptive parents' rejection as I was of my birth mother's.

The strange thing about my search and being adopted was that I had never read a single book on adoption. I read every other kind of self-help book, but it was so instilled in me that adoption shouldn't be an issue. Although my insides screamed out for some identification, I simply went along with the accepted wisdom.

About four days after I mailed the letter, I came home to a ringing telephone. I unlocked my door quickly and lunged for the phone. It was Alice Clarkson, and she talked very fast in an excited voice while I listened as hard as I could. 'Yes, your mother is delighted! She really wants to meet you. She knew one day you would search. Her children have never been told so she needs some time to tell them. Her husband always knew . . . she would love to meet you straight away, but the problem is she has relatives coming to stay and then the whole family are going to Italy for three weeks. So it would be best we waited until they get back . . . Would you write her a letter and send her a photo?'

I was thrilled and amazed. I asked more questions, like, 'What did she sound like?' and 'Are you sure she was really happy to hear from me?'

I felt a bit disappointed that she wouldn't meet me for a while. It was strange that she too, like my adoptive parents, had a holiday booked just as I showed up. Nevertheless, I think in this case I was relieved. Letter writing, for the moment, felt safe. I asked the social worker what I should write and she advised me to keep it simple; I didn't need to tell my whole life story yet; there would be plenty of time for that.

I do remember sitting down to write the letter. I stared at the blank page for a long time. I was writing to my birth mother and it didn't feel real. How should I word things? What do you say to a stranger who happens to be your mother? I kept the letter very brief. I think I told her what I was up to in my life, but I didn't go into any details about my emotional state. I thought it wise to save that stuff for later! I spent ages choosing a photo to enclose. After all, I wanted to look really good! I ended up sending one from a holiday when I was tanned and my hair had just been blow-dried. She didn't need to know I was back to my pale-faced self; she'd find that out soon enough.

I received a letter back soon after. As I held the envelope in my hand, I began to shake; more than anything else, I wanted to see what she looked like. I ripped the letter open. Enclosed was a recent Polaroid photo of her. I think Pat too had just blow-dried her hair and she was smiling in a nervous way. It struck me that whoever had taken the picture was joking with her about something, trying to get her to relax. I studied the photo for a long time. I looked at it in different lights, even taking it to my window so that I could see her as clearly as possible. She wasn't what I had expected.

But what had I expected? A two-headed freak? A disfigured face? I didn't really know, but I could see the similarity between us straight away. She looked so young, so normal. There I was again, saying *normal* as if it was a strange thing. Whatever I expected, it wasn't *normal.* Looking back, I believe it was because I was seeing a reflection of myself for the first time, and I had no real concept of what I truly looked like. And deep inside me was the belief that my mother had given me away because I was ugly, that in some way I was disfigured.

I opened the letter and began to read.

> *Dear Zara,*
>
> *Thank you for your letter and photograph.*
>
> *You're a beautiful girl, but I knew you would be. You were such a beautiful baby.*
>
> *I've always hoped that one day you would contact me, but now it's happened, I can't quite believe it. Since I spoke with the social worker I can't seem to stop crying.*
>
> *I felt extremely nervous and apprehensive at the thought of meeting this stranger who happens to be my daughter, but on seeing your photograph, I can see that you are not a stranger but someone who is very familiar to me.*

She described her family and then told me that she wouldn't be able to meet me for a while, as she was going on holiday for three weeks. Once again, I marvelled that my introduction to both my mothers was delayed by their holidays.

We exchanged a few more letters before she went away and I learned a little about my brother and sister. She also told me about how she met my birth father, that he'd been a student working in Soho as a waiter and they had met at a club called Les Enfants Terribles.

Dear Zara,

You can imagine my parents' shock. "Nice Jewish girls" just did not get pregnant. I was sent to a mother-and-babies home in Finchley, and after you were born I was meant to stay at the home until you were six weeks old. Unfortunately, the day after you came back, I became ill and I was rushed back into hospital. You were then placed with foster parents, and I only saw you once more when I had to take you to the court to sign adoption papers.

It's always been my deepest regret that I could not keep you, but I was a very immature seventeen-year-old and without the support of my parents I would never have managed.

I adore my children but there's always been something missing in my life. No child can replace another.

Love,
Pat

Some of the words were comforting: that she had wanted to keep me meant so much, yet it was still truly hard for me to understand why she hadn't. I could not at that time put myself in her shoes. I longed for more detail about my birth father, but it all seemed rather vague and I was too scared to ask for more. I was very guarded and unsure of how to be.

I know this sounds crazy, but I had never really thought about my birth father before I met my birth mother. Now

I don't want you to think I had ideas that I was the product of immaculate conception (well, maybe it did cross my mind). I just never thought about him. As a child, all I focused on was my mother. It was only when I received my birth records at age twenty-four that I began to realise, 'Oh yes, there had to be a man involved in this somewhere.' I had always felt like I was planted on the earth somehow, that I didn't arrive like other people did.

I must say that finding out he was Italian felt great to me. I always had a thing for Italy and thought the women quite stylish. Well, let's face it, Italy has gorgeous clothes. As soon as I found out I was Italian, I immediately remembered an incident from a few years earlier with my adoptive mother. I had always liked crosses. I never thought of them in a religious sense. They were spiritual symbols to me. I had a huge wooden cross hanging in my bathroom and a smaller cross with rosary beads that I had bought at the Vatican. All the time I was unaware that I was half Italian.

My mother popped over to my flat and went to use the bathroom. The next thing I heard was a big howl. 'How could you!' she shrieked. It took me a moment to realise that it was the cross that she was mad about and I reassured her that it meant nothing as far as religion went; I just liked it. She was very upset and believed it was a great insult to Judaism. I had not meant to offend anyone; I just felt very drawn toward it and kept saying, 'It's from Italy, the Vatican in Italy. It is just a reminder of the power Italy had for me.'

My girlfriend Melanie, who had worked with me with Geldof, came over to take me out a few nights later. As I came out the front door, she said, 'My, aren't we looking Italian today?' We laughed a lot, but it felt so good, so freeing. The funny thing was that we had worked together as backing singers and we had toured Italy. The whole time we were there I kept complaining about how crazy the people were and that I didn't understand why they had to shout so much. And all the time I was one of them.

Melanie flew me to Italy later on that year as a birthday present. She was working there as a backing singer with Duran Duran. Most women would have been thrilled with the prospect of hanging out with those boys. I was simply thrilled to be in the country I now knew I was connected to. It was wonderful to be back in Italy, knowing who I was. It was a very different experience. I looked at everyone in the street, at their features, their colouring and I could see the similarities. An old man started chatting with us – well, flirting, actually – in a market, and he asked us where we were from. We said London and then I happily told him I was half-Italian, which made him laugh and pinch my cheeks. I laughed too. All the questions I had carried for so long and the emptiness of not knowing had slowly begun to fill up.

11
Reunion

Becoming pregnant the first time brought my search to the forefront. It had always been something I would do some day until I got pregnant. It took me eight more years to complete but I knew I would never give up until I found the answers to my questions for my children and myself. Jeanne

I met my birth mother at the end of the summer of 1988. She telephoned the social worker and we set up a meeting at Alice's office, which was walking distance from my flat. The night before I went into complete panic and obsessed about what to wear. There it was again – my old friend Appearance Obsession. It gave me a false sense of control, and of course I had to look acceptable so that I wouldn't be rejected. I believed that looking good would help cover up all the turmoil inside.

On the day of the meeting, I walked slowly up the street noticing my every breath, my every step. I wanted to be very dramatic and thought about all the movies I had seen where long-lost relatives see each other for the first time. I imagined a camera crew filming me and wondered if I was reacting in the right way. After all, I was about to meet my birth mother and I was sure that one took on a certain look for that role.

I looked at everyone I passed on the street, just people going about their business, running for a bus or grabbing a newspaper. I wanted to stop them and say, 'Hey, do you notice how different I look today? I am going to meet Her, the woman who gave birth to me, the woman I have imagined since the day I was told as a young child that I had been given up for reasons that still don't really make sense to me.'

Nobody seemed to notice me as I walked more and more slowly. As I finally arrived at the office, all the bravado that had carried me there crumpled. I wasn't in a movie. This was real. I began to have a panic attack. I vaguely remember Alice Clarkson taking my arm and leading me up the stairs. My mother, she said, was already there. My breathing got more shallow and I muttered, 'No, wait! I can't!' But she didn't listen and before I knew it, she had opened a door. I turned around and there were my birth mother and her husband.

They both stood up. The husband, with tears streaming down his face, hugged me and I began to cry. My birth mother, dry eyed, hadn't moved. I walked over to her and kissed her, and we all sat down. Then they all began to talk at once. I just sat, unable to speak. I felt numb. I was glad for their chatter because it gave me time to glance at her, to study her. I thought how different she looked from what I had thought my mother would look like. I couldn't tell at that time whether she was attractive or not. I saw a lot of similarities between us; it was different from looking at a photo. Her mannerisms were so much like mine: the way she dressed, the jewellery she wore, it was so much my taste. She looked very well put together and I could tell she took great pride in her clothes. I wondered if she had worried about what to wear as much as I had. I noticed her shoes. Very stylish, I thought, and her feet weren't particularly big, so I didn't get that from her. Mine had always been exceptionally large, which caused me great anguish. I saw that her body type was just like mine too: she was slim and in good shape with olive skin much like mine. I was, however, a good few inches taller than she, which surprised me a little.

We sat for I don't know how long. I remember thinking how green the room was and how much it needed a good paint job. I sat alone on a big faded armchair that had lost its spring. I didn't want anyone near me at all. My birth mother sat to my right on a hard-backed chair that made her sit stiffly upright. She seemed so contained, so in control of her emotions, yet I sensed that a lot was brimming underneath.

I liked that I could sink back into my chair. Its big arms around me gave me a feeling of safety and a place to hide the tears that constantly streamed down my face. I felt ashamed of them, and I wished that she too would cry so I wouldn't be alone with my feelings.

My mother's husband sat off to the left, not quite in the group, and I continued to watch as they talked to the social worker, who did her best to keep the conversation going. I was still unable to speak. Nothing felt real. If I could just watch like an observer I would make it through. 'I will think about it all later,' I told myself, hoping to distance myself and stop my tears. I didn't want to linger too long on any feelings. I felt so vulnerable and I wished I had someone with me.

The social worker, thinking she had to be a social worker, kept asking us questions, like 'How do you feel?' and 'Isn't this incredible?' I felt mainly numb. After a while, we decided to go and have some lunch.

We went to a local restaurant. Despite the gravity of the situation, my primary emotion was guilt. What if someone I knew came into the restaurant, or worse, a friend of my family? Even though I knew in my head that that I had every right to know my heritage, in my gut there always lurked a feeling of betrayal towards my adoptive parents.

Once inside the restaurant I felt a little more relaxed and the tears stopped. I began to listen eagerly as my birth mother told me about the family. She talked a lot, which was exactly what I wanted. I needed to know as many details as possible. She told me that she had revealed me to my brother and sister and that both had reacted differently. My sister Roberta was excited but upset that she hadn't been told before; my brother, Orlando, on the other hand, took one look at his mother's serious face and thought she had killed his cat. He was so relieved to know the cat was all right that all he said when she told him about me was, 'Oh, OK,' and carried on with what he had been doing. Everyone thought this was extremely amusing, but I wasn't quite sure what to make of it.

Over lunch, we made arrangements for me to visit their house to meet Orlando and Roberta. They gave me directions, not knowing that I had already been there. After an hour or so, we finally parted. I was relieved to get back to my place and be alone.

I won't bore you with all the times I have met with my birth family because over the last twenty years there have been many. I will highlight only the occasions that have had most impact – those days that left me just barely making it out of their house, waving happily goodbye and then howling uncontrollably all the way home. They have seen me cry, but the howling I prefer to do in private.

I was extremely ignorant of what it meant to reunite. I had no idea at all of the emotions that would arise from all the parties involved; my expectations were extremely high, even though I told others that they weren't. How could they not be?

With hindsight I realise that I genuinely believed that somehow meeting my birth mother would make me whole, that she would be able to fix all the pain. All the years would tumble away and all my problems within myself would be solved and vanish. I know this sounds incredibly naive but I have found that I am not alone with this feeling. Adopted people who never got to meet their birth parents, either through death or not wanting a reunion, ask me, 'How will I ever get through that phase, that fantasy?' Those who are adopted live in fantasy. If no one gives you instructions or a map, how do you know how to play the game? I had no map and no knowledge of how this adoption story would work out. I felt like a child inside although I kept up my front so that no one could see what I truly felt.

I had no idea when I met Pat that she would want me to fix *her*; that she saw me as some kind of saviour who would mend the hole she had suffered all these years; that just by reuniting we would both feel complete. I couldn't believe it. After all, I was the baby coming back and she my mother. Don't mothers nurture and love their child unconditionally? Yes, most mothers do with their baby but how do you do that with an adult? We both had expectations of each other that were far too high and too unrealistic, but no one warned us.

I first met Orlando and Roberta about a week after my introduction to my birth mother and her husband. It felt strange to drive to their house knowing that this time I would be going in. I was nervous and excited at the thought of meeting my siblings. I parked outside, took a long, deep breath and knocked on the door. Pat and my sister opened it together. Roberta and I looked at each other, smiled and said, 'Hello!' I felt instant connection and fondness, pure and uncomplicated. We were both awkward, and giggling seemed to ease the moment. Roberta looked like me: round cheeks, similar eyes and eyebrows, which I noticed straight away. I was good at analysing faces – I had done it for years. Picking out the similarities in the faces of biological relatives' faces had almost become a pastime.

I longed for me and Roberta to be alone together, to find out who she was, but years would pass before we had that opportunity. Pat always wanted to be with us. I liked that my siblings were half-Italian; it gave us more in common. Nevertheless, I felt safe with Roberta – wherever I went on that visit, whatever room I walked into, she was always close behind me and wasn't shy to sit right next to me on the sofa.

My giggles soon turned to tears as I walked into the kitchen and saw my twelve-year-old brother, Orlando. He sat on the counter, covering his face with his hands. I think he was crying and my tears began to flow and flow. Gosh, how I hated that part of myself! I wanted to stop, to pull myself together, but my tear ducts had a will of their own, and my birth family was unsure of how to respond. They just pretended it wasn't happening and began to chat away. They pulled me into the living room and the next thing I knew I had my sister and mother on either side of me pulling out photo album after photo album, showing me in pictures their whole lives: my mother getting married, the growing-up years of the children, holidays, all the normal family stuff, yet to me it was fascinating. I studied each photo; I especially loved the ones of my siblings as babies. They were so cute! I felt immediate connection to both of them and I also felt surprisingly protective. Suddenly I was taking on the role of big sister, which was so strange after being the youngest in my adoptive family. I was also shown pictures of great-grandparents and uncles and told about my ethnic heritage. I had Russian, Austrian and Dutch blood on my birth mother's side, and my father, of course, had been Italian. No wonder I had felt confused at times!

My birth mother went through photos of me as a baby growing up. She had asked me to bring them but I sensed that, for her, looking at them was really painful. I also showed her my adoption file and she read it all. There was a part that showed letters describing my development which were meant for her eyes, but Pat said she never received them. We concluded that her parents must have kept them from her. She had been given only one photo of me, which she had kept.

She said that what they had written about my birth father wanting to marry her was simply not true; social services had wanted to make it all look nicer than it was. Maybe that's an English thing or maybe it made me more acceptable for adoption. After all, who wanted a baby that may have come from bad blood or who might turn out to have too many problems? But I had so needed to believe that my parents wanted to marry each other. It was another fantasy that I had to let go of and it hurt immensely.

My grandparents soon arrived. My grandfather walked in saying loud hellos and kissing his grandchildren. My grandmother came in quietly behind him. I was still sitting on the sofa with the piles of photo albums, feeling, let's say, just a little overwhelmed. He took one look at me and said, 'So you're the skeleton in our closet!' What does one say to that? More relatives arrived later that day: the great-uncles who had sheltered my birth mother during her pregnancy, along with their wives, one of whom bought me a welcome present that made me cry again; and my birth mother's brother, the one who had answered the phone the day I had been born and was told 'It's a girl.' He had kept that knowledge to himself until he had been told about me only a few days before.

Somehow I made it through the afternoon. Luckily, they are a chatty family, so I could sit back and observe. I felt my grandmother staring at me the whole time, yet every time I looked over at her, she looked away. They all told me how much I resembled Pat.

I watched my brother and sister interact with their grandparents and their mother. I could see the shared connection that comes only with years of being a family, years of history with one another, and waves of sadness crashed over me. I would never have that connection with them; those years were truly gone. As Pat had missed watching me grow, I had missed seeing my siblings grow, and I still felt like an outsider. Paradoxically, reunion helped in many ways to fill the void, but in other ways it made the void bigger than ever.

I left that day, as I did many times after our first few meetings, relieved to be alone in my car, to have a break from the onslaught of emotions that came and went. As soon as I had turned the street corner, I began to cry, then howl. A sound like the cry of a wounded animal exploded from me. It was powerful and terrifying, yet I knew that howl had been buried within me since the day Pat gave me away. Somehow the heart remembers even when the undeveloped brain cannot. The devastation of losing my mother, the grief that went unhealed, here it all was, overtaking me like the floodwaters from a broken dam. I wanted to see them, to be with my family, yet when I was with them, I felt as though the pain would drown me.

I was invited out to dinner to celebrate Pat's and her husband's wedding anniversary. Roberta and Orlando and Pat's brother and his wife picked me up. We all met at a Japanese restaurant. Each table had a little cooker upon which the waiter prepared our food as he showed off his culinary skills: he held the cooking oil way above his head and poured it slowly into a tiny pot, then cut vegetables at great speed, which I found highly irritating.

Wine was ordered. Normally that would not have bothered me, but that night it was very difficult. It wasn't that I wanted to drink – I just didn't want to be around the smell, to observe the subtle (and sometimes not so subtle) changes that come over people as they drink. I felt vulnerable and alone and I longed to be sitting with my recovery friends having a cup of tea and a laugh within the safety of that circle.

One of the presents my brother and sister gave to their

parents was a specially framed photo of themselves when they were small. I felt the ominous welling of tears. Yet again I was reminded that they were connected and I was not. Once more I felt the deep sadness at not having known my siblings as young children, that those years were gone, and that I had missed their lives.

At that moment, the waiter began to cook in alcohol the food I had ordered. He was pouring it on, and when I told him that I didn't want alcohol on my food, he assured me it would burn off. He poured more on; again I told him I didn't want it. The rest of the family told me it was no big deal, that I wouldn't taste it. I was only in my second year of sobriety and still scared of the power of alcohol. I didn't want it near me, so I mustered all my strength to repeat that I didn't want it cooked on my food. Against my will I began to cry and couldn't stop. It was as if the flood gates had finally opened and I had no control at all. I felt all the sadness of all the years of not knowing my birth mother, the pure loss, the lack of connection I felt to either of my families, the sorrow of missing my brother and sister, the pain of sitting together finally and them being strangers to me. The tears kept falling even though I shouted inside my head, 'Stop! It's enough already!' Everyone at the table carried on talking as if it wasn't happening. They too were embarrassed by what was happening to me. I think Pat asked me once if I was OK. Finally I made it to the bathroom where I locked myself in and howled. I wanted to leave right then but I had no car and no money.

Pat found me. She had assumed it was all about the waiter not listening to me, but I couldn't find the words to explain; there was just too much. Finally I persuaded them to drop me home, and the relief I felt when I entered my flat was overwhelming. I was safe.

The next morning, Pat called to say, 'Thanks a lot for ruining my evening.' I was devastated and, for me, the relationship was never the same again. I knew in that moment it would never be the way I had dreamed. There was too much baggage. I just hadn't expected Pat to be angry with me for having the feelings I did. At that time, it was too much for her to recognise my own loss, that it's not something that birth mothers have a monopoly on.

When I tried to explain the loss I felt, how overwhelmed I was, her response was 'What about me? Didn't you think it was hard for me? The past is over. Let's be happy now we are all together, let's just get on with the future and enjoy now.' I wish it could have been that simple. For a while I tried to fake it, but those feelings kept rising up within me as I began to get in touch with things I hadn't known were there.

There have been two occasions when communication was broken off for extended periods, once for two years and the other for a year. Both times each of us wanted the other to understand where we were coming from. We each needed the other to take away the pain and we couldn't, which only made us angrier at each other. Perhaps we were angry too that, instead of a fairy-tale happy ending, meeting each other only brought up feelings made more potent by having been stuffed down for so long. We were both victims of circumstance and I was crushed that she couldn't be the mother I had dreamed about. It had been just another fantasy.

One month after I met my birth mother, a very dear childhood friend gave birth to her first child, a daughter. I was very excited and drove to the hospital as soon as I got the telephone call. I burst into the room, about to deliver congratulations and a big hello when I abruptly had to change pace: calmness enveloped me, and with it, the energy and peace that only a newborn can bring into the world. I was unsure of what to say and I felt like an intruder. My friend's mother sat in a chair watching her new granddaughter. My friend and her husband were on the bed, Gina lying down and David sitting next to her. The baby lay between them. Although they glanced up for a moment to greet me, they were clearly mesmerised and returned their attention to the baby. They imitated the face she made as she tried to focus on her new surroundings, they touched her face and hands, inspecting her all over as though they couldn't believe that she was real.

All this time I stood quietly by the bed, half hidden by the curtain that they had now pulled back. I just watched. Until that moment, I had never witnessed the connection between mother and baby. I had never thought of my friend as someone who cared especially for children, yet there she was with her own baby, the impulse and response to motherhood showing me a side of her I had never seen before. Unexpectedly, tears began to surface along with an ache in my chest. My lightness of mood began to fade. I tried to make conversation with Gina's mother, but felt she was just being kind, that secretly she felt I was intruding on a sacred time for the family. I wanted to leave straight away, but waited a while in case they thought I was acting strangely. When I could contain myself no longer, I left, saying I would return in a day or so.

I walked quickly to the lift and out of the hospital. I was relieved when I found my little blue car waiting for me. I started the engine and was ready to pull away when I stopped and pulled up the brake. A howl erupted from my throat, tears flowed as though they had no end. At last I began to make the connection, a feeling both uncertain and familiar: my own birth had been nothing like what I just witnessed – no joy, no celebration, no awe, just a frightened, lonely girl and an infant who would soon be parted from her.

12
Breaking the silence

I would just love to look my birth mother in the face, but my adoptive mother would be crushed. She's all alone in this world other than our family. I have not begun my search so as not to crush her. Helen

I was twenty-four years old at the time of my reunion, but emotionally I was very young, still carrying all my childhood feelings around my adoption. I still hadn't had any support from any professionals in the adoption field.

When I found my birth mother, I was too afraid to tell any of my adoptive family. I kept it to myself, sharing what I was going through only with close friends. Everything felt so overwhelming, so extreme, so powerful and at times debilitating that I could deal with only one stage at a time. I remembered the occasions when my adoptive mother had told me that she would help me search, but that she would be hurt if I did. Other times when we discussed my adoption, I felt that she was waiting for me to show that I wasn't really interested.

For two years I stayed silent, sometimes visiting both families on the same day, especially if it was a holiday. Each time, I felt the burden of a secret life but I was crippled with fear. I simply couldn't find the strength to tell them. In fact, I had sworn to my friend Simon, who was helping me, that I would never ever tell them, that it would devastate them, that they didn't need to know. Yet as the months went by, it became harder and harder to juggle my double life, and I was haunted by guilt. What if they found out from somebody else?

At last, about two years after my reunion with my birth mother, I had another revelation: I was driving over to see my adoptive family when it suddenly struck me that my terrible fear wasn't all about me protecting them. The truth was I was terrified that they would reject me, that they would no longer want me as their daughter. I was a grown woman of twenty-six, yet feeling just like that vulnerable child again.

The following Sunday morning I woke up knowing that today was the day. I don't know why it happened that particular day; somehow my body just couldn't contain the secret any more. I needed to be free from it. I spoke to Simon and he said, 'Well, it seems like you can't wait another day. You need to do it now. It will be OK.' My emotions were overwhelming and the tears wouldn't stop. Once again, I was a young child with no anchor. Trembling with an adrenalin rush, I called my parents and told them through my tears I had to come over and tell them something. I was barely able to speak.

I feel so bad over the way I handled it. My parents were so worried. They had no clue and they later told me their imaginations conjured up all kinds of terrible things. I drove straight over, praying to God all the way to help me. I found my parents waiting by the window, looking extremely anxious. The moment I walked in, I blurted it out, 'I've found my birth mother!'

No one said much at first, but eventually my mother began to ask questions. I told them I had known Pat for a while. They were surprised and didn't understand why I hadn't told them sooner. Why now? Why was I so upset? I didn't know how to answer because I couldn't tell them the truth: that I remembered every incident, every word, every look from my adoptive mother when the subject had come up during my childhood and that, even though we hadn't discussed it in years, her reluctance had affected me deeply. The fact that I was now an adult didn't make any difference to my feelings. I kept silent.

My mother asked to see pictures and I showed them. It felt very strange. Even though my blood relatives were so connected to me, there was no similarity between the two families. Pat was almost a different generation from my adoptive parents – sixteen years younger – and their lifestyles were not similar at all.

Mum asked about my birth father. I told them the story and that he was Italian, to which my mother replied, 'Yes, we know he was.'

I felt as if I had been hit in the pit of my stomach with a bowling ball. My head began to swim. 'You knew?' I whispered. I couldn't believe that they had known and never told me. I felt so much anger and shock, yet again I sat and stared at the floor in silence. Then I noticed that my father was sitting the same way, silently staring down to the floor. He hadn't uttered a single word.

I left their house that night feeling very different from when I arrived. I was exhausted and relieved, yet more importantly, I felt more grounded, as if I was finally stepping into my own body. It felt good. At last I had done it. The secret was out and I knew then that how my parents chose to deal with this information was up to them. I simply couldn't carry it all any longer. I had to stop protecting their feelings. They were, after all, grown-ups. It was time for me to heal my sadness and anger, to stop being a victim of this situation, to move on with my life.

13
A new life in LA

My daughter is the only person I feel a total connection with in the whole world. Felicia

I was twenty-eight years old and I had finally reached a place within myself where I was happy with my life. I had recently moved out of my little bedsit into a new flat with low rent that would be mine for as long as I wanted to live there. It gave me a feeling of security that I hadn't had before.

At last I had stopped obsessing over whether I would marry and start my own family. There were so many other things I could do with my life, and I knew I would rather be alone than in a crazy relationship. Nevertheless, I was exhausted with the burden of keeping so many secrets for so many years and constantly protecting my adoptive family and my birth family so that nobody got hurt.

I had a friend named Shelly who had moved to California some years earlier and we kept in touch. She encouraged me to move on with my life and come over for a visit. I had no obligations to hold me back, so why shouldn't I take a vacation? The idea of getting away for a while was very enticing.

I arrived in Los Angeles in December 1993 and Shelly met me at the airport. What a dramatic change! I'd left London in the fog and cold, and stepped off the plane onto what might have been a different planet. The sun sparkled and everywhere I looked, flowers bloomed. I couldn't believe how spacious it all seemed and how clean. The sky was so big and there were so many palm trees. Of course I wanted to do all the tourist things that people do when they first visit the West Coast but I was happy just to be in different surroundings.

A few days into my trip, I was sitting with a group of people I had just met through my friend. We were talking about England and they were asking me about life over there. Everyone was ever so friendly and welcoming. A guy walked into the room wearing what looked like clown pants and a T-shirt and he was extremely loud. My first thought was, 'Who the hell does he think he is? And why is he wearing those ghastly trousers? What an ego!'

Clown Pants came over and shook my hand. 'I'm Jonathan,' he said warmly. As I looked into his eyes, I saw a certain gentleness there. Suddenly, I felt that I knew him, that we had met before. The group decided to go out to dinner and I was invited along. We ended up at Bob's Big Boy, a very old and famous burger place on Riverside in Toluca Lake. 'Wow!' I thought, 'A real American diner, just like in Twin Peaks.' Jonathan ended up next to me and I placed my bag between us. 'Don't worry,' he said with a smile and a twinkle in his eye, 'You're safe sitting with me.'

At first, I listened as everyone else talked. Then they asked me questions about London and what life was like there. They were a merry bunch, people enjoying life, and I realised how serious we could be at times back home. Life could indeed be fun. And did these people know how to laugh! They offered precisely the kind of nourishment that I had been missing. I also knew that I wanted to get to know this American, Jonathan, more.

Two weeks later, I had to go back to London. I didn't want to leave, but I was armed with new ideas to take to my friends and a new attitude that I wanted to hang onto. I also wanted to nurture the hope that I had been exposed to. It would be so easy to fall back into the old ways again and I was tired of it. I didn't want to go back to old thinking and negativity. It was time to move forward.

I had already decided that I would return to LA and spend more time there, but first I had to tie up a few things back home and earn some money. During my time back in London, I kept in regular contact with all my new friends, including Jonathan. I was convinced that he would forget about me the moment I left for London, so I was always surprised when he called.

For six months, I worked as hard as I could, waitressing, babysitting, anything to make some money. My closest girlfriend, Carol, told me later that I never really came back to London. She could see that I was already gone, and that no matter how often I said I would be back in a year, she knew that I wouldn't.

Leave-taking has always been extremely difficult for me, even if there is no tension in the parting. It is hard to trust that, even though we separate, I really will see loved ones again, that they will always remember me. It seems to reactivate an old anxiety. At the airport, when all my adoptive family and friends came to see me off, I realised how frightened I was of leaving them all. I knew my life was going to change dramatically and, even though we had our problems, they were my family and would be there for me in whatever ways they could.

Mum handed me a beautiful letter telling me how much she loved me and would miss me. It was very healing because our relationship was still extremely complicated and strained. She knew I wasn't coming back, something I also knew in my gut, but I couldn't face it right then. I cried all the way to LA, which was very embarrassing, as I was seated next to an elderly American couple who thought what I needed was a nice chat about what the US was like. I did my best to control my inexhaustible sobs, but they soon gave up and I was left to weep in peace.

Arriving back in LA was suddenly terribly scary. This time, I wasn't going to be there for just two weeks. I had decided to stay a year and that suddenly felt like an extremely long time. There were major challenges, like where I was going to live and how I would earn a living. There was also the culture shock factor: I began to realise that speaking the same language didn't mean there weren't quite a few differences between the Californians and the English. We are brought up so differently. Americans are much more patriotic, take a more open view of life and seem to talk more openly and easily. Total strangers actually said 'Hello' as I walked past them on the street, something that rarely happens in a big city like London. I was always surprised when someone said a big cheery 'Good morning!' I was used to being ignored and avoiding eye contact.

Then, of course, there were the basic everyday difficulties, such as the first time I tried to post a letter and couldn't work out where the slot was on the post box. I found myself walking round and around, quite baffled as to how to get the letter sent, when I finally figured out that you had to lift the handle! I felt so embarrassed, convinced that dozens of people had been watching me and thought me a total imbecile.

The accent caused a difficulty too. No one seemed to understand when I asked for a glass of "water" and it took me time to feel comfortable saying the word with an American accent. One time I was terribly thirsty, and I took the four-year-old boy whom I was taking care of into a shop with me. I asked for a bottle of water and no one understood. I mimicked water coming out of a tap. The man stared blankly. Finally I looked down at my little charge and said, 'Please help me. Can you tell him what I need?'

'Sure,' he said. 'She wants water.' I got my drink.

I did, though, enjoy the attention I got just for having a British accent. Everyone would talk to me and no matter what I said, they appeared to find me interesting. It seemed that every time I went shopping someone would ask me if I knew their friend George or Sammy from London. I tried to explain that, even though London is small compared to the US, there are a lot of people living there and I was sorry that I really hadn't met their friend. But it didn't faze people – they just wanted to talk to me.

It took time to make friends so I was pleased to help out when one of my new American friends organised a group that regularly visited a local AIDS hospice and asked me to come with them and sing. I was happy to be asked but more than a little nervous. Still I went ahead and at the end of the evening I had signed up to join the group. The hospice became part of my weekly life and on the days when I was most homesick and feeling alone, I would visit my patients. It was incredibly fulfilling to participate in this group and I remained a regular until the place was closed a year later. I also began to gather some musicians together to start playing in LA. I hung out with all my new friends, including Jonathan, as much as I could. We would all sit in Jonathan's house and chat into the small hours as we got to know each other. The two of us were rarely left alone. There seemed to be safety in numbers.

It was during these informal social gatherings that more of my "stuff" began to surface. My new friends asked questions about my life. I told them that I was adopted and that I had met my birth mother. As I began to talk about it and saw they were truly listening intently, I felt such emotion rise into my chest that I knew I was about to break down. If I let my feelings out, it would be loud and ugly and I would have no control. This felt very uncomfortable, especially since I was trying to impress a man. I couldn't understand why this was happening. Surely I had dealt with all of that. People would look at me, waiting for more explanations, and I would get up and run out of the room, leaving them to puzzle over what had happened and where I had gone. As for me, I couldn't explain what was going on inside or what it was connected to. All I knew was that the feelings seemed harder and harder to contain.

This happened a few times. I had never felt emotions on that level before and I didn't trust anyone enough to let them see these feelings surface. Nevertheless, I began to get an inkling of how much unresolved stuff I still had to deal with. Miss Recovery wasn't as recovered as she had hoped.

Jonathan and I would go for long drives in the mountains. It was very romantic and we would talk for hours. Jonathan showed me all of LA. We went to the movies a lot, something we both enjoyed. Nevertheless, we decided not to become lovers and to just get to know each other as friends. For me, sex always clouded my reality. Once it was brought into the equation, the relationship was either over or based solely on sex, and I had promised myself I wouldn't do that to myself again. So I tried to get to know Jonathan, to see who he really was and to allow him to see me, warts and all. I had never stayed around long enough to do that before. Yet who would have thought that just sitting and being with someone you cared about could bring up so many intense feelings – mainly fear? For the first time, I began to see my fear of intimacy. I had no idea how to be authentic, to behave without the sexual lure. I had always pointed my finger at the man, saying he was the one who was unable to commit, when the truth was it was I who couldn't.

I couldn't shake off the feeling that I had known Jonathan before. We both realised we had never actually met, yet there was something strangely familiar about him that I found comforting. I felt drawn to his enthusiasm for life, his spirit. We began to discover that we shared similar interests, that we both wanted certain things in life. We also had a lot of fun. I began to see that Jonathan liked me for me. Up until then, naive and immature as I was, I had based my whole romantic life on sexual attraction. What I learned is that in married life sex is only a small part of the package.

When Jonathan began to talk about marriage, I freaked out. 'I can't get married,' I said.

'Why not?' he asked. 'Do you have a secret husband you've forgotten to tell me about?'

I laughed. 'I just can't.'

Jonathan managed to look confused and amused at the same time. And I had no idea why I thought I couldn't get married. Eventually, he gave up talking about it, although he did wonder out loud whether I wanted to spend my life flitting from one relationship to another without truly committing or taking the risk. Ouch. That hurt. I knew it was true, yet I was terrified. I wasn't even sure what of.

Gradually, I began to realise that I truly trusted Jonathan, something I'd never felt with a man before. That was extremely important to me. I cannot say specifically how it happened. I just watched how he lived his life. He was consistent with me, he kept promises as best he could and was gentle and kind, not only to me but to others. Naturally, like everyone else, he had his dark side too, but it didn't seem to bring him down. He could snap out of a bad patch and his view would always turn to the positive. That was something I wanted; I liked that he trusted life's process. I wanted to strive for that, to know not just in my head, but deep inside, that it was OK to enjoy life.

Most important, I felt loved. That indeed is an incredibly healing gift. I had been so afraid to let my defences down, to feel love or be loved, and I knew that really I was lonely and wanted to share my life with another person. And here he was. I wasn't going to let fear sabotage my chance at happiness.

We got engaged in December 1994 and that's when I started acting out more of my adoption stuff. Poor bloke – Jonathan must have thought he was going to marry a psycho. We would have a lovely day together and then I would create some argument and tell him to leave. In fact, I remember pushing him away, saying, 'Just leave, you are going to sooner or later, so why don't we just get it over with?' He took a lot, he tells me now, because he knew I was just scared. I think he deserves a medal for bravery and tolerance.

Moving in with him was hard. I remember asking him if we could change some pictures around, which at first he didn't take to kindly, because they were his beloved car photos. But I didn't want them in every room of the house. We had a debate but soon worked out an agreement. Nevertheless, I felt terrified that he would ask me to leave because it wasn't really my house and I should be grateful that he'd been willing for me to move in. I began to remember that as a child I had had the same feeling. If I clashed with my parents, I worried that they would send me back to the adoption agency.

14
Marriage

*I doubt I would ever have had children had I not been
married to a man who wanted them very much. I had the not
uncommon adoptee's feeling that I had never been born, so
how could I give birth?* Zoe

I have heard it said many times that the most stressful
events in life are marriage, moving, having babies and
divorce, so I decided to choose three of those major life
changes in a very short space of time. First, we got married
in London. At the same time, we packed up my flat. It was
a terribly exciting time, yet scary and painful too. The way
I dealt with it was by not actually saying goodbye to
England. I told myself that for now we were going to live in
America, but that we might be back in London at any time.

I was very glad to change my name to Jonathan's and
within a couple of weeks of marriage had switched all my
documents to my new surname. As an adopted person, I
had grown up with a name I liked very much, but I always
knew it really wasn't who I was. I was somebody else, I just
didn't know who. After meeting my birth mother, I knew
half my genetic lineage but, to this day, the paternal half is

a mystery. My surname never gave me a feeling of wholeness because it wasn't who I started off as. I have heard parents say, 'That's my boy! He's a Smith down to the ground' or 'She's my daughter all right, just like my side of the family.' Well, I didn't feel like anybody's side of the family, so taking on a new name felt wonderful. I felt as if, for the first time, I could be who I really was; I belonged to this name and my own family was going to start now.

Getting married was a lot of fun. I can see why people do it over and over again. The dressing up, the make-up, the hair . . . I was in pure heaven being the centre of attention, plus of course, the excitement of becoming a wife. My mother was thrilled and, I feel, a little relieved that I was finally settling down and she did a great job of organising the event.

Since Jonathan and I were of different religions, we got married in a register office. It was in a beautiful, very old brick building surrounded by gardens. It also featured a large driveway with plenty of room for the wedding car to drive up. Normally in a register office wedding, the entire wedding party has to wait outside and walk in together, but I really wanted to walk in last. As it was a quiet day of the week (Tuesday, July 4th, 1995), my husband-to-be and his friends (who had flown over to be his best men and support) spoke to the women in charge and asked if I could enter last so that Jonathan would not see me ahead of time. At first they were a little flustered and in awe of these handsome Americans. They said they couldn't promise, but just then a friend of mine arrived, who was a popular actress in the TV series Emmerdale Farm. The officials were so excited to meet her that they soon made a place for me to hide so that Jonathan and I couldn't see one another.

I waited in a small office with my dear friend Carol, my dad and a little girl for whom I'd babysat. My grand entrance was so much fun. Even though it was not a religious service, the love of all the people I cared about filled the room with a beautiful spiritual presence. After the ceremony, we went off to dinner and dancing. On each table there were British and American flags. What a fine time we had! Part of me wished that my birth family could have been there too, but it would have been too hard for my parents, and I didn't want that day spoiled with strained feelings. In an ideal world, both my families would have come together.

We had our honeymoon in Stratford-upon-Avon, which for Jonathan was very exciting as he loves Shakespeare. Stratford is a magical place. The streets, the houses and the countryside all around are truly picturesque and there is so much to see. We explored almost every part of the town, visiting museums and Shakespeare's house. We even sat together on the bench where Will and his girlfriend, Anne Hathaway, had sat when they were courting.

One afternoon as we walked along a canal, I suddenly had the strongest feeling of being pregnant. I actually wasn't at that time, but I spent the whole day in a state of exquisite warmth, as though I was surrounded and protected inside a bubble, or that I existed in another dimension from all the hundreds of people walking past. My belly felt full and I experienced a contentedness I had never known. I wanted the feeling to last forever. I was almost embarrassed to tell Jonathan, who always became slightly nervous when I mentioned babies. He wasn't quite ready at the time, and wanted to do the provider bit of having money and a job – all the sensible things.

The next day, as we walked through the town, a total stranger rushed up to us and gave us tickets for a bus tour. He was unable to use them and would we like them? We thanked him profusely and he disappeared back into the crowded street. When we looked at the tickets, there were actually three of them. Later the same day, we went into a museum. The man at the ticket counter became irritated when three tickets instead of the two we requested popped out of the machine. 'This has never happened to me before,' he grumbled.

We had decided before we got married that we would wait about a year before starting a family. On the plane back to America we whittled it down to six months. But once we got home the visitations, as I like to call them, became even stronger. I had a constant feeling that Jonathan and I weren't alone anymore, that there was someone else present. The feeling got so intense that I knew I couldn't wait any longer. I told Jonathan as we were driving home in LA that I felt right then and there as if an entity, a powerful energy, were in my womb and that this baby was so ready that I was finding it hard to argue. But I wanted Jonathan to be ready too; I wanted him to want the baby as much as I did. Our baby had to be consciously desired by both of us, conceived with a mutual commitment, not a surprise or the result of a careless night of passion.

A week later, my husband told me he was now ready. Suddenly I panicked. I'd never been pregnant before. What if I couldn't conceive? Jonathan looked at me gently and said, 'Zara, I feel like if I breathed on you, you would get pregnant.' He was right. I was pregnant six weeks after the wedding.

15
Motherhood

*Being adopted is part of what makes me who I am. I have
three sons and it was just as wonderful and exciting each time
I gave birth – to look upon their small faces that were part of
me like nobody I had known before, to feel I belonged to
someone and they belonged to me.* Jackie

Motherhood is an incredible miracle. What I didn't expect
was how it awakened parts of my self that had long been
dormant or perhaps had not even been there to begin with.
Mainly, it has got me in touch with the most terrifying
emotions I, as an adopted woman, could ever experience:
love, intimacy and the inevitable that will one day happen
in some form or another, loss. I had never before allowed
myself to really love. It is true that I fell deeply in love with
my husband, but I can always find ways within my
marriage of keeping distance, putting up walls. With my
beautiful children this has been impossible. I have never
loved with such tenacity or felt such depth of emotion, nor
had I ever before got in touch with the true effects of my
adoption, mainly feelings of loss and sadness that I had
suppressed my entire life. It seems that giving birth to my

children was also a birth for my whole self.

On the night our first child was conceived, I knew instantly I was pregnant. Later, though, I was assailed by doubt. I had terrible cramping in my stomach. I went to a midwife for a blood test, but it came back negative. I was so upset. I had felt so sure. A few days later, I did a home test while Jonathan was out. I was so nervous that I ended up peeing all over the stick and dropping it down the toilet. I decided to wait until my husband returned home and was outside working on his car. This time I did it the right way. I waited, holding my breath, and clear enough, two pink lines appeared. At that point I felt as though I'd flown out of my body. Jonathan tells me I came floating out of the house, waving the stick and muttering that I thought I was pregnant but wasn't really sure. Could he check it just in case? He came into the house very quickly, took one look at the two pink lines and declared, 'You're pregnant!'

'Are you sure?' I asked. He pointed to the picture on the box and then at the stick, which by this point had two deep red lines that looked as if they had been drawn with indelible marker. 'Two lines,' he said patiently, pointing at the diagram and looking at me as if I couldn't speak English. 'Two lines,' he repeated emphatically, pointing at the stick. 'Watch my lips, Zara. You are pregnant and I have no job and the car won't start!' We both stopped and caught our breath. We were pregnant. We were ecstatic.

I did another test later that day and then another first thing the next morning, 'just in case,' I explained to Jonathan.

'In case what?'

'In case it goes away,' I replied lamely.

I booked an appointment with my doctor, who said he would do a blood test to be sure, but that the home tests were pretty accurate. The blood test came back positive. I finally began to believe that, yes, I really was pregnant. I, Zara, an adopted woman, was able to get pregnant and have my own child. I had never felt that I would be allowed.

I wasn't working at the time of my pregnancy, just waiting for immigration papers to come through. I couldn't actually leave the country, which left me very uneasy. What if something should happen to my family and I couldn't go home? Getting married to an American was not as straightforward as I had thought. There was a lot of red tape and we had to wait a year-and-a-half for the interview to prove that our marriage was legal. I spent much of my time rehearsing with a band and writing songs. I had a lot to say, and it became a joke when every week I turned up with another new song. 'Wow,' my bass player would say, 'you really are on a roll with this pregnancy thing.'

I missed my family a lot during this time, especially my mother, but I was also aware of how I didn't want to talk too much about being pregnant to her. This was something she had never experienced and, automatically, I began to protect her.

Pregnancy is a strange state of being. The first time, for me, was so daunting because, let's face it, you have absolutely no idea what is going to happen or how you're going to feel. Yet at the same time, once I knew I was pregnant, it felt completely right. Somehow, everything I had ever done in my life made sense because it had led me to this place of marriage and pregnancy. Everything else seemed totally irrelevant.

I am a fearful person who likes to control everything – I mean everything. How other people feel, what is going to happen next year, how to keep everyone happy and liking me. I have been known to take great risks so that I can maintain the illusion that I am in control. Then I got pregnant and lo and behold! I had absolutely no say in any of it. My tummy began to expand. I began to crave oranges and muffins and went to great lengths to make sure I had my supply. As a veteran of various addictions, I was very good at feeding my needs. I spent many wonderful hours in the Aroma Café, downing blueberry muffins and taking a few home.

I enjoyed the changes in my body. I marvelled at the fact that this little being knew just how to grow. At the appropriate number of weeks, he grew toes and toenails and little fingers. How did he know how to do that? I realised that in spite of what I ate or thought, my baby was just going to keep on growing until the day he decided to be born. There was nothing I could do to persuade him to come out any sooner.

As someone adopted about to become a mother, I had no real idea that this state was like standing on the edge of an active volcano. A fountain of lava was about to erupt from its depths, spilling out all its contents with no warning. Four months earlier, I had started therapy with a woman called Marlou Russell. Adopted herself, she specialised in adoption work. Thank goodness for her. It was such a relief to me to know that I was not alone in all the feelings I had and that many of them were common for adopted people.

I began to read everything I could find on adoption. It amazes me that, prior to starting therapy, I had never done it. I think it was my way of believing the myth that I was really OK. After all, I had two parents and I'd been told often enough how lucky I was, and how grateful I should be. My therapist gave me great reading materials and suggestions. I was so hungry to read them that often, when I left her, I could barely wait to get home. I would try to look at them while driving and then howl all the way home. Feelings, more intense and primal than anything I'd experienced before, began to stir deep within me. They were somehow familiar and the tears and grief that I had carried for so long felt almost comforting.

I was a few months pregnant when I started having experiences of what I later learned was my own birth. They would often happen in the night. I would wake up and feel as though an entity was trying to leave my body. It was like a huge round boulder that crept up slowly from somewhere deep within. Then it would begin to try and spiral out of me. I would try to ignore it, but I felt as if I was going to burst open. I would sit up in bed and begin to cry softly. Then as the energy of the boulder reached my throat, my voice would go higher and higher and louder and louder and I would feel myself whizzing through a long tunnel. But every time I saw the end, I felt tremendous fear. I'd get up and pace around, saying, 'No, no, I am not ready for this.' I would never allow myself to pass through to the other side. If I did, I would surely die. I knew, though, that this experience was connected to my self as a baby; being pregnant became the doorway to finally getting in touch with those feelings.

Jonathan would wake up and somehow figure out what was going on. Then he would hold me, which was hard for me to allow him to do. I would lean back on him and he would reassure me, telling me it was safe to go through what I needed to and that I would be OK. Today he tells me that the sounds he heard were like those of a baby. For me, it was intense and frightening because they were so primal. During these episodes, I had no control, yet each time it happened, I would try to go a little further.

I phoned Marlou. 'Is this normal?' I asked, a little embarrassed. She assured me that even though it wasn't common, it did sometimes happen. She advised me to allow the process to develop. It even had a name: cellular memory. The body remembers experiences from before we even have words. I thought it was going to kill me.

I had never heard the term cellular memory before I attended adoption workshops, but I now realise it is something I have experienced all my life. There are books for those who want to examine the subject in depth (see Resources at the back of this book), but for now, I will explain the concept as briefly and simply as I can.

It is believed that as the cells are being knitted together to form a new human life, before there are language and words, memories are formed of the time in utero. Whether it was a good experience or a bad one, whether the mother was overjoyed or contemplating abortion, the baby picks up those feelings. They remain with us inside our bodies in the form of physical memory. It is becoming common knowledge that babies in the womb respond to music, light and sound, so it makes sense that a baby would also respond to its mother's stresses and joys.

For most of us, these memories are very deeply suppressed and the emotions surface only when the individual is exposed to situations that trigger them, such as the severing of important relationships. For people who have been adopted, getting married and having babies can jump-start the feelings. Questions start to formulate and the body remembers.

I felt a great sense of relief when this was finally explained to me. All my life, I had felt as if I was battling to prevent a force within me from surfacing, something so dreadful that it would surely devour me. In certain situations – sometimes just hearing a baby cry – I would slide into a pit of black despair that I didn't understand. As a child, I loved films about animals, yet if there was a death or separation involved, I would have to leave the room. My parents would find me sobbing, sometimes uncontrollably, and the depression and sadness would swallow me again.

Further along in my pregnancy, I began to have dreams of birth. I never actually saw myself give birth, however. It was always the next day; I'd show up at the hospital, walk up to the nurse's station and tell them I had come to collect my baby, but I had no idea what my baby looked liked or what sex it was.

Pregnancy is a vulnerable time for women. I worried the whole way through, always thinking that I would either lose the baby or that there would be something wrong with him.

I just couldn't grasp that I, like thousands of generations of women before me, could give birth at the end of nine months. You may call it self-obsession and in a way it was. I believed that for me it would be different, it wouldn't be a normal experience, something would go wrong.

I regularly met other pregnant women at an exercise class. We would chat about our visits to the obstetrician while we awkwardly mounted bicycles and pedalled as best we could with our expanding bellies. 'My baby is huge, I hope I can get it out,' or 'I can't stop eating chocolate! I have put on fifty pounds and I'm only seven months pregnant.' And then hysterical laughter as one of us tried to get up from the floor after doing our Kegel exercises. It was fun, but I often found myself studying these women, looking for signs of their feelings. Nobody mentioned her fears and I wanted desperately to tell them how I felt, that the reason I was extra tired that day was because I had been up for a couple of hours rebirthing and howling the night before. But I didn't feel that I could throw that into general conversation, so I just smiled my way through the classes and kept everything hidden.

One day at the end of class, one of the women finished a chat with a woman who appeared to be in her late thirties. She had just had a baby, but she didn't seem like it. She was a little distant and there was none of the elation or joy that I would have expected from someone who had just given birth. After she left, the other woman turned to the rest of us and said, 'That woman did the most selfless act a human being could do.' We all looked at her expectantly. 'She gave her baby to her brother because his wife couldn't have children. Isn't that wonderful? He is so happy.'

I felt as though ice water had been poured down my back. Everyone else agreed, while I suddenly felt sick to my very core and intensely angry. In the space of a second, I went through a maelstrom of feeling for that poor baby. I wanted to shout, 'You're all nuts! What about that baby?

Have you considered how he might be feeling? Don't you know that it's going to affect his whole life? How could she do such a thing?' But I never uttered a word. I just walked away, leaving the girls still talking. 'What we need are more women in the world like her.'

I had just finished watching *Seven*, about a psychopath who kills everybody and delivers the head of Brad Pitt's girlfriend to him in a box. Do not ask me why, at nine months pregnant, I chose to watch that film. I still had a week before my due date but I had drunk castor oil, as I had heard it would help get the baby moving. I decided to have a cup of tea and walked into the kitchen. Suddenly water started running down my legs, and I thought, 'Oh great! Now I am incontinent.' I paged Jonathan and he called back quickly. 'Water keeps coming out of me,' I told him. 'Your waters broke,' he replied.

'I don't know. Do you think so?' I had gone into a weird space and felt very detached from everything. Jonathan came home immediately and called the hospital. They told him to bring me in straight away. I had had some mild contractions earlier, but now I began to have stronger ones. 'I don't need to go,' I protested. 'They'll just check me and send me home.' Jonathan gave me a strange look but said nothing. Instead, he got the bag, the one they tell you to prepare ahead of time to take to the hospital.

'Why are you getting the bag?' I demanded. 'I won't need it.'

Jonathan turned to me again. This time he smiled nervously. 'Zara, you are going to have a baby.'

'I'll bet you I am not today,' I said.

He didn't argue. 'Get in the car,' he said, taking the bag.

'We won't need it,' I repeated.

Once at the hospital, they put a wristband on me and admitted me. I glanced at my husband with surprise. He smiled back, knowing that it was in his best interest not to say, 'I told you so.'

Even though Jonathan stayed with me the whole time, I was terrified and it was a long labour. I wanted to go drug free, but I began to wonder whether I was brave or just stupid. The baby got stuck. Finally, after three hours of pushing, they suctioned him out. Suddenly, a lot of people came rushing into the room but I wasn't sure why. The doctor wanted to get the baby breathing, so she didn't hand him to me right away, but I saw that it was a boy. I looked over anxiously to where people were helping him. 'Is he OK?' I asked. After what seemed an eon of time, I heard a cry. 'He's fine!' someone reassured me. Moments later, they handed him to me all wrapped up in a soft little blanket. I stared at his face in awe and then at Jonathan, whose eyes caught mine and then fastened in amazement on our son. 'Hello,' I said. 'I'm your mummy.' He stared back.

At last, he was here, my baby boy! I had felt throughout the whole pregnancy that I was carrying a boy. When I looked at baby clothes, I looked only at boys' things, thinking boys' thoughts. I was delighted that my intuition had been right.

When I was pregnant, I visited a bookshop to look at colour pictures of a baby in its mother's womb at different stages. I would check the appropriate month and stare at that strange-looking creature with bud arms and a large head and I would weep right there in the bookshop, imagining my baby and thinking how beautiful he was. I even had a dream that when my baby was presented to me, he was a little monster with two heads and strange eyes. Yet I fell instantly in love with him, and I knew then that I would love my baby no matter what.

After a few minutes, the doctors wanted to whisk him off for a bath. I was seized with panic, afraid he would be taken away from me. I told Jonathan to go with them, to hold the baby and never, not even for one instant, take his eyes off him. I said it over and over. My poor husband must have felt that I thought he was an imbecile, but he was beginning to get an understanding of my irrational fear.

Once Zach was back from his bath, I was able to relax and I felt a contentedness I had never experienced before. I held him for a long time and then we decided to count his toes. We all stayed the night in the hospital. Once, the nurses came in and said, 'Let us take him to the nursery so you can get some sleep. He's so lovely, the girls will adore him.' 'No way,' I said. 'He's not going anywhere without me.' So we spent the night with Zach asleep on me and I nursed him. I hardly slept; I just wanted to look at him. I couldn't believe he was real. Jonathan and I took turns holding Zach, dozing off occasionally, and enjoying the privacy of our little hospital room. The next morning we took our son home.

16
Fear

I remember going to the hospital with anxiety and great fear. I wouldn't get out of the car. I said I had to wait for a contraction. Last year, twenty-three years later, I realised I hadn't wanted to go to the hospital because I'd thought they would take the baby away, that I would lose her. Treva

I had looked after many children and babies in my life before Zach came along, so I really believed that mothering wouldn't be that difficult. I felt I had some understanding of children, but I was in for a big surprise. No matter how much I loved those other children, nothing could have prepared me for the overwhelming feelings that the arrival of my own baby brought. I had had no clue whatsoever and the power of these emotions was frightening.

I felt so overwhelmed, so inadequate, that I didn't know how to express myself. My psyche, however, appeared to know exactly how. One night, when Zach was about six weeks old, I sat up in bed sweating, shaking and crying. I had dreamed that Zach had been taken from me. A strange man grabbed him and ran away. I woke in such a state of confusion that I believed that it had really happened. I went into the lounge where Zach and Jonathan lay sleeping in order to let me rest. I saw that Zach was safe, but I couldn't stop crying. Jonathan assured me over and over. 'It's just a dream, Zara, it's not real!' It took all night for the feeling and visual memory of the nightmare to fade.

That nightmare was the first of many I suffered in the first few months of my son's life. The theme was always the same: my son was taken from me, sometimes by a man, sometimes a woman, and I searched for him frantically. I always awoke before I found him. The depth of grief I experienced in these dreams was what I should imagine a mother would feel if her child had died – they were truly unbearable. I have to say that in my entire period of sobriety up to that point, I had never felt so strongly the need to numb myself. Thankfully, this period passed and my sobriety remained intact.

I understand it is not uncommon for new mothers, adopted or not, to experience such fears. With time, I began to realise the origin of my own nightmares: as a child, I had continually looked for my mother on every street. I always knew that she was out there, I just didn't know where. It was I who had been snatched away by someone unknown to me.

I could never leave my son, not even for an instant. I would do the normal things that mothers do, checking to see if he was breathing and so on, but what I never told anyone was that I went to his room to make sure he was still there. I always feared that he would just disappear into thin air. Of course, it never made any rational sense – he was in a room with no way of getting out – but I kept checking nonetheless. In the end, I decided to have him with me at all times. I never told Jonathan the truth of the matter until much later. I was afraid that if I revealed too much, I would be sent to a doctor who would find me an incompetent mother and take the baby away.

One day, when Zach was only a few weeks old, my husband and I had a silly argument. I was left feeling that

Jonathan and Zach were eyeing me critically. I felt sure my son was assessing whether or not I was doing well as a mother. I stood apart from them, feeling ganged up against, when Jonathan looked at me and said, 'Zara, this is your home. We are not going to throw you out.' I was amazed. 'How did he know that?' I wondered. I'd spent my whole life growing up waiting for my parents to tell me to leave and now, as an adult woman in my own home, I still felt that eventually they would cast me out, that I didn't have the same rights as everyone else.

To this day, the fears I have about my children being taken can get out of control. I am learning to stop the scenario and scream, 'Go away!' or 'Fuck straight off and stop ruining my life!' But my, how they like to persist, especially when everyone is getting along well, and more especially when I stop in the middle of playing with my children or holding them tightly as they go to sleep. I take in the moment and feel a love that I have never felt for another human being. I often tell them how much I love them, how happy I am to have them. Often in these tender moments my eyes fill up with tears and my children will look at me, a little unsure. 'Mummy, are you crying again? 'Why are your eyes watering?' I tell them it's because I'm happy and proud. 'You're weird,' my daughter will reply.

Twelve-step programmes had literally saved my life, but in California I discovered adoption support groups, something that I'd never encountered before. When Zach was about nine months old, Marlou suggested that I attend some meetings of a group called CUB (Concerned United Birthparents). It had been started by a group of birth mothers, but adopted people were welcomed. CUB helped me a lot in understanding Pat. I had never met any other birth mothers before and, even though it was insightful, at first, it wasn't easy to be around them. I was angry and didn't want to hear their excuses for why they gave up their babies. It took years for me to accept what had happened to these women and how their lives had been controlled, how they had been victimised and received no support from their families. I truly believed that if I had got pregnant, no matter what the circumstances, I would never have made that decision.

I needed a place where there were just people who had been adopted so that we could talk freely without the worry of hurting anyone's feelings and a group of us started to meet on a regular basis. These meetings weren't all serious; sometimes we'd get quite hysterical as we shared things about our common experiences. We talked about how, on a first visit, doctors always ask about hereditary diseases and who in your family is living and who has died, and how, when filling out medical forms, we sometimes just made up illnesses and families. Some people wrote in huge letters 'ADOPTED', depending if they wanted others to know about their adoption status. We laughed, too, about the kind of fantasies we had – one friend was convinced for years that her mother was Roseanne Barr!

At last I had found people coping with abandonment and loss issues that are specific to adoption, and I felt comfortable just sitting in the same room and listening to their stories. I wasn't crazy after all. I wasn't the only one who experienced fear about loss and guilt towards their adoptive parents. I was relieved that it seemed very common. Adoption is an emotional subject and the problems don't end with reunion. In some ways, reunion is just the beginning of the road.

17
Understanding

I became more aware of my feelings about being adopted after [my babies] were born. I had suppressed them for many years and having children of my own made me confront them and finally start saying that I was entitled to those feelings. Before, I had always worried about everyone else's feelings and pushed aside my own. Maggie

Many years ago, I saw a television programme involving women who, at an early age, had lost their mothers. The pain and the grief they endured as they grew up were devastating and their stories upset me a lot. The reason I could identify with these women is that, growing up, I too felt as though my mother had died. This was horribly conflicting since, after all, I had a mother. I never told anyone of these feelings – it wouldn't have made any sense. The worst part was that I didn't know if my birth mother was alive or dead, so I lived in a state of constant unresolved grief, always searching for her. Though most of the time it was subconscious, I have read that, just as there is no closure for the families of soldiers missing in action, there is no closure for the person who has been adopted.

My adoptive mother mothered me as best she could: she treated me as her own. I in turn loved her. She was the only mother of whom I had any memory. Unfortunately for us both, she didn't know that adopted babies grieve no matter how much you love them, feed them, kiss them and cuddle them. The adoptive mother is not the mother they want. Through no fault on my mother's part, I never really trusted the relationship. I always felt afraid I would be rejected again, that maybe she didn't really like me, that I wasn't the right daughter for her after all, that if she had had her own biological daughter they would have had a better relationship. It has taken me years to understand the complexities of this issue, and now that I have children of my own, it is becoming clearer than ever what we – my adoptive mother, my birth mother and I – missed out on.

In her book, *The Primal Wound*, Nancy Verrier describes in detail the complexities of the relationship between adopted people and their adoptive mothers. Nancy adopted a baby and has a biological daughter. Even though she adopted her baby very soon after birth, she could see the differences in how the two babies bonded: the adopted baby simply didn't connect with her in the way her "natural" daughter did. It was with extreme relief that I read this book and began to let go of the guilt I had felt about how I had behaved towards my adoptive mother. I had always blamed myself for the conflicts we had but, as I read, I began to see that it wasn't my fault. I had no idea of why my situation was so challenging because no one had ever told me.

When Zach was a year old, I wanted to know more about where I had been during the first weeks of my life. I wondered about the woman who had fostered me. I hadn't thought much about being fostered before I had him – I was "only a baby", it wasn't that important – but thought about those early weeks with him, how much I had totally fallen in love with my baby and how well I knew him. I remembered Zach's first smile, his recognition of me, his mother, how much he had changed and grown and the routine we had established, how we were getting to know each other.

One afternoon, I lay down for a nap. Suddenly I found myself thinking about my foster mother and I had another powerful cellular memory experience. There were no words for it, since it emerged from a time before I had language. It came to me with amazing clarity: I was crying for my foster mother, not because it had been a bad time but because it had been good. I wept because I realised I had bonded with her and leaving her had been, once again, devastating. Not long afterwards, I managed to find my foster mother and we spoke on the phone and exchanged a few letters. She was incredibly warm and down to earth and filled me in on those early weeks when I lived with her. It was another important piece of information.

After Zach was born, my mother came over to visit. He was just six weeks old. This is about the age that many babies are adopted, so for adopted women who are new mothers, a lot of old grief can be triggered. It can be expressed consciously or unconsciously. Subsequently, I was in a very emotional place when my mother visited. Having a baby, as most women know, is the biggest life change one can undergo. In addition, I was having those nightmares and cellular memories that I couldn't put into words, so being around my mother was hard. I wasn't able to express all that I was feeling because I was still trying to protect her. I found myself feeling guilty for being able to have a baby so easily, for being able to breastfeed, and I began for the first time to really understand the loss my adoptive mother must have felt from not having her own child. I was terribly sad for her and realised that she had missed out greatly – we both had – and there was nothing I could do to change that. I could never be her natural daughter and I could never make her feel better about that loss. Guilt is a strange waste of time in the cold light of day. It made no sense at all to feel guilty for not looking like my mother, or for being able to conceive a child. Nevertheless, the guilt had always been there. I just didn't realise it until Zach was born.

I remember looking at my son. I couldn't believe how much he resembled my husband. I was told that he also looked like me, but that was harder for me to see. I notice how much strangers like to talk about whom the baby looks like and am thrilled when they perceive the resemblance. But on a deeper level I know him, I understand his stubbornness, his ability to play imaginary games, the way he loves to run fast, his likes and dislikes. I understand when he throws a tantrum. He is so much like me.

'Oh no,' I pray, 'Please let him have an easier time than I did. Please let him not take everything so sensitively that he can barely function. Please don't let him believe that he will be forgotten or lost forever. I pray he has more self-esteem than I did.' And then I am quieted by a voice that says, 'Zara, he knows who his mum and dad are.' 'Oh yes,' I think, 'he won't be spending his childhood looking for a stranger who might bear some resemblance to himself.'

One evening when Zach was barely a few weeks old, I lay on the bed with him. He had just started smiling, which, as any new mother knows, is total bliss, especially when you've had no sleep for nights on end. Babies just seem to know when that magical time for a smile and a coo should come. I wanted to stay awake and watch him forever. 'You are perfect,' I whispered, 'just the way you are.' In that moment I knew without a shadow of a doubt that I, Zara, wasn't a mistake – that no baby could possibly be a mistake. I was meant to be here, to be the mother of this child. For me to keep thinking that I had been a mistake meant that he was too and I knew that couldn't possibly be true.

18
The missing link

My baby has enormous blue eyes that could only be from my side. According to my [birth] information, my birth father had blue eyes, so I assume that's where they're from. They are her most remarkable feature and the most talked about and commented upon. It's a constant reminder of the unknown.
Xaviera

I never understood until recently that it's possible to miss what you never had. Many times, as Jonathan, Zach and I lay in bed at night, Jonathan would tell me stories of his father. He had contracted Alzheimer's disease when my husband was just a teenager. He died twelve years later, but Jonathan has fond memories of his father and speaks of him often. On one particular night, listening to him talk about his father and then about being a father, I realised I felt almost jealous that, even though he had lost his father, at least Jonathan knew who he was and had been able to spend time with him. I began to cry deeply and found myself uttering, 'I miss my father.' The words surprised me. I had never really been aware of the feeling and somehow it felt good to be in touch with the truth – so freeing to say out loud that I do miss him; I miss not knowing what he looks like, who he is, what kind of man he is, and that although his relationship (if you could call it that) with Pat was fleeting, it doesn't make any difference to me. I still would like to know who he is as much as I wanted to know my birth mother.

A few years ago, I decided to find the club, Les Enfants Terribles, where my birth parents had met. My girlfriend in London took it upon herself to find it. The place had changed names but was still the same as it had been in the Sixties. When I went back to visit London, I walked up and down those streets. When I eventually found the club, I couldn't believe it. With my husband and son standing beside me, I peered through the window, pressing my nose against the glass, trying to see inside. I was disappointed because it was closed for refurbishing. Just as we were about to walk away, the door opened and a workman came out. 'Do you want to go inside and look around?' he asked. I was delighted. I walked down the stairs and found myself in a smallish room with low ceilings, red walls and lots of tables. This was, I was informed, where all the Italians used to meet up in the Sixties to hang out and socialise. I could easily imagine what it had been like, full of young people chatting, drinking, smoking.

I stayed there for a while and tried to imagine Pat and my birth father meeting. I savoured the moment. This was the closest I had ever been to my birth father, standing in a room in which he had also stood. Later, I walked up and down to all the Italian restaurants and barbers in the area with flyers and questions to see if anyone might have known this man, Vittorio, waving back and forth to Zach while he waited outside with Jonathan. But with no surname it was impossible. I knew it was a long shot, but as someone adopted, I couldn't just sit back and do nothing. I had to try and satisfy that part of myself.

After I found the place where they had met, I walked

through the neighbourhood with Pat, hoping it would jolt some further memory. But she stayed mainly silent except to reaffirm that she didn't know anything. She had no more memories. As we sat down to have lunch, I began to feel resigned that the effort had been useless. Just as we were leaving, though, she asked, 'Would you like to see the area where he worked?' 'Of course,' I said. We walked through Soho, away from Wardour Street into Piccadilly Circus where she pointed at a narrow street. 'I think he worked down there,' she said, 'but I am not sure. It's the direction he went one evening. Would you like to see where we waited for a ride from our friends?'

We strolled to an area bustling with people and stood for a few moments in the spot they had stood. I imagined the two of them, how young they were, and felt as though I had been given something of him.

One Italian man responded to an advert I placed in an Italian newspaper. He was around the same age as my birth father, and he too used to hang out at Les Enfants Terribles. He told me that although he didn't remember ever knowing my birth father, he would be glad to meet up with me and give me suggestions. I was very nervous – after all, I had no idea who he was. We met in a restaurant and I found myself studying his face, part of me hoping he really was Vittorio and was just checking me out. He told me a lot about the club and what it had been like in those days. I began to get more of a picture in my mind and it helped fill in a little piece. I was grateful for his kindness. I also met with the local Italian priest, but to no avail.

I continue to go through my frustration of not knowing. I still wish that Pat would willingly help me on my quest, but she won't. I have to bring up the subject or it is never spoken about. This has left me feeling betrayed. I really believed that Pat more than anyone would understand my need and do anything to help. I didn't understand that she would have so many feelings about my birth father and in other ways, no feelings at all. From her perspective, she was the only parent who was important. She couldn't accept my need to know and I couldn't understand her attitude about it. This has caused great rifts in our relationship.

Recently, I asked her again (this time, without any anger) and I told her the truth: that I had been having a difficult time not knowing, that sometimes I look at my children and think it doesn't matter. At other times it matters so much that I can hardly bear it. I felt her listen and she has promised me that she will look into some things and see if she can help. I sensed a shift in her attitude.

There is, however, yet another mystery surrounding Vittorio. Patricia met her husband, Franco, when she was twenty-one. Her parents were not happy as he was also Italian and he wasn't welcomed into the family at first. It wasn't until her parents understood that they were serious about getting married that they accepted him.

Pat and Franco moved into a large house split into bedsits, where many other couples lived. Pat didn't know any of her neighbours very well. Around the time of Roberta's birth, an Italian couple told Franco that they knew Pat had had a baby a few years earlier and had given it away. Pat had told Franco about me before they were married. It had been around my birthday and he had found her crying. She said she had to tell him the truth, that she couldn't marry him keeping such a secret.

When I met Franco, he said that he, too, had thought about me all these years and that he thought of me as a daughter. He was always very kind; once he looked at my hands and said, 'You have Italian hands.' Pat was extremely surprised that these people knew about her earlier pregnancy, since she had told only one friend. She tells me news travels in the Italian community, and we have wondered for years how that couple knew. Perhaps they had been friends of my father.

I still wonder about my birth father and, irrational as it sounds, I still look for him on the street, sometimes catching the eye of a man about his age and imagining that is what he looks like. Recently, we were flying back from London and there were a couple of Italian men on the plane in front of us. I found myself smiling and staring at them and they at me. I'm sure Jonathan thought I was just eyeing them up but I found myself studying their faces, just in case they were my brothers. I like hearing Italians speak and watching how they interact.

I will never stop looking. I can't. It's an automatic reflex, and whether I will ever know him is a mystery. I don't have the illusion that he could fix me, but it would feel exhilarating to see his face.

19
Healing and loss

Motherhood is the most healing thing. To have the intimacy and the connection and to look at her and see reflections of myself are profound. Her personality is like mine and I just know her. Gayle

Home is supremely important to me, as it always has been. I am not someone who never unpacks. I need my belongings around me for comfort and security. I have been able for the first time within a meaningful relationship to let the walls down, to let my husband see who the real Zara is. It is truly terrifying even today to show that side to another human being, but, thank goodness, harder still to keep it all inside. When you live with another person, he or she tends to notice (if they're not on drugs, that is) when you feel sad or mad.

In the past, I dealt with my emotions very differently, especially with boyfriends. When I began to search for my birth mother, for example, I was dating an actor. This seemed fun at the time. While I was seeing him, I had my meeting with the social worker, found out my birth mother's name and sent off for my birth records. I hadn't said a word to him. One day he came over to see me and I was being my usual aloof self, which translated as 'I am so freaked out and I feel like crying. Best not to show it.'

I casually mentioned that maybe he had noticed I had been a little distant recently, to which he replied, 'Yes, you're always a little distant.' I asked him if he wanted to know why.

'OK,' he replied calmly.

I loved drama, so I took a deep breath. 'I just found out who my birth mother is. I know her name.'

His mouth fell open. 'You have been doing this and you *never* told me?' He was truly shocked. 'Well, duh,' he said, 'no wonder you have been a little distant.'

I looked at him and replied with a small smile, 'Or maybe I'm just as good an actor as you.'

Even after years in recovery, I still experienced tremendous discomfort in certain situations. For example, if I read or saw anything about babies or children being lost or taken from their parents, I became nauseous or felt an energy that filled my stomach and made breathing difficult. The fear that these sensations would envelop me caused me to find ways to turn them off: I avoided the subject or busied myself with something else so I wouldn't have to see what lurked beneath those feelings. I believed that they were somehow part of who I was.

When Zach was two years old, I had a miscarriage. I was ten weeks pregnant. At a routine check-up, my doctor couldn't detect any heartbeat. In a way, I wasn't surprised; I hadn't felt a connection with the baby. At the time I got pregnant, I was scared to have another child. In retrospect, I understand that although I wanted more children, I was still resolving a lot of issues and needed more time. Yet everyone kept asking and I had felt pressured somehow into creating the perfect family with the perfect age difference.

One morning, a couple of weeks before the miscarriage,

as I drove home from dropping Zach at school, I suddenly felt an extremely powerful presence all around me, an energy that seemed to circle my head. I was certain that it was my baby. I began to weep as I drove, saying, 'I don't want you to go, but if you have to, I won't try to stop you.' Although I cannot explain how, I knew with unalterable certainty that its little soul had chosen to leave. I told no one, not even Jonathan. I thought he would chalk it up to me being a worrier. I went straight into denial and carried on as if I were still pregnant. Yet I began to feel too good, too normal again. My body stopped changing.

Later, I had the fateful ultrasound. Even though somewhere inside I had known all along, my conscious mind did not want to take it in. I stared blankly at my doctor. 'What do you mean, there's no baby? Are you sure?' She looked me directly in the eye and repeated, 'There is no baby. I am sorry. It just didn't develop properly.'

I left her office sobbing and called Jonathan from the freeway. He left work and met me at the house. The feeling of emptiness enveloped me. It was so strange. One minute you're pregnant and the next, you're not. I couldn't get my mind around it at first. The emotional pain was extremely intense. I would try to rationalise that the baby wasn't really a baby. After all, I had been only ten weeks pregnant.

Next came guilt: the baby had left me because I was in conflict and it must have been confused by my emotions. I had an image of it saying, 'I am not hanging around here with this crazy mother! I'm off to find one with more emotional balance.' I also felt guilty that my body was somehow defective. Maybe I had eaten something bad for me; perhaps I hadn't taken good enough care of myself.

I really hoped that I would just get over it. After all, miscarriages happen all the time. Yet I was amazed at all the women who, when hearing about it, came forward to reveal their own. I began to see that losing a baby was almost as much a secret as abortion. Women hid their grief, yet most of them never forgot their feelings and still thought of those pregnancies. In some ways, miscarriage is as much an unrecognised trauma as relinquishing a baby.

Although we never spoke of it, my mother had suffered several miscarriages. I knew they were the reason my brother and I had come into our parents' lives. Now I thought of my mother with a new sense of compassion, not only for her but for all infertile women. How devastating to go through all the work of taking temperatures, having examinations, only to learn that your body, for whatever reason, is unable to carry a child to term. I reminded myself of how blessed I already was to have our son.

Many women who'd told me about their own miscarriages said that they had got pregnant again very quickly. I hoped for that too – I wanted that awful pain of emptiness to disappear – but deep down I knew I wasn't ready. I couldn't force myself to heal. I had to go through the process of grief and mourning and learn their painful lessons.

My miscarriage triggered deep feelings around loss and shattered the fragile trust that I had begun to develop. I had felt the rug pulled out from under my feet. I couldn't believe that it had happened to me. I had to confront the harsh truth that I didn't trust nearly as much as I had hoped. All that work and my faith went straight out the window as soon as I lost the new baby. Worse, I felt incredible fear. What else was going to happen? What else would be snatched away from me? I began to slide down that dark slope into depression.

I realised that I had to rebuild my foundation. I had a choice about how to see my life: I could look only at the negative or I could emphasise the positive. It took all the energy I could muster to accept that my miscarriage had happened for a reason. It caused me to question my faith, something that would ultimately deepen and strengthen my spiritual development. I also had to accept that I do not recover from emotional injuries quickly. I have to work through my feelings bit by bit. No shortcuts.

A few months after my miscarriage, Jonathan and I went out to dinner. I said, 'I feel like I am just sitting around waiting to get pregnant, counting the days, disappointed each month. It's no good for me. I need to write about my experiences as an adoptee having my own child. It's time to write down all those feelings I had with Zach, and I want to find out if other mothers who were adopted feel like me.' The more I talked, the more I began to feel really excited at the prospect of compiling a book. I was suddenly aware that I had a purpose: all the pain would be worth it, having been adopted would be worth it if I could tell my story and help others.

Later, I buried the baby book that I had started under a new tree that Zach and I planted together. It was my way of recognising the miscarriage and the life that had briefly resided within me. After we had finished the planting, I sat back on my heels quietly looking at the tree. Zach sat quietly next to me. He put his hand on my knee and said, 'Don't worry. Mummy, she will come back again.' Six months later I was pregnant with my first daughter, quickly followed by our second. Did 'she', as Zach predicted, come back again after all?

20
Someone who looks like me

My second daughter and I looked so much alike as babies, I almost felt like I had been replaced. It was really odd to have someone look like me. I was so bonded with my daughter for that, it almost scared me. Tanya

I was pregnant again. Could it be true? I wanted to doubt it, so I did two tests just to make sure. Nevertheless, there it was in front of me, those two red lines. *Wow!* I was filled with delight, then fear. What if I had another miscarriage? What if I carried another child to term? What if it was a girl?

That overwhelmed me – a girl, a daughter, a mother–daughter relationship. I was afraid, yet so excited. And that day was my birthday, a day I never looked forward to. A day that had always been filled with difficult emotions could be different now. My feelings were all over the place. What a gift! My birthday would never be the same again.

My feelings of fear around having a girl stemmed from the fact that my adoptive mother and I had never really got along. We both tried so hard and there is no denying the love between us, yet we have always been mismatched. We just never connected easily; we really didn't understand each other; for years, just having a conversation was difficult. Our opinions, our interests, our taste in clothes are as different as they could be. Many people who aren't adopted tell me they feel different from their mothers too, but genes play a big part. The longer I am a mother, the more I am conscious of this. I felt myself beginning to change: I had to remember that I deserved wonderful things. I had a right, just like other women, to have more children. It was a whole new mindset.

Months later, my son decided he wanted to watch the men who were assembling some furniture we had just bought for the baby. I was hugely pregnant, only a few more weeks to go, and pottering around the house. I could hear Zach from the other room chatting away to the workmen. He is a very friendly boy and never has trouble talking to people – so different from how I was as a child. I never enjoyed speaking to grown-ups, especially people I didn't know.

My son brought in his toolbox to show the workmen what he had and then I heard him say proudly, 'My mum is just like Superman!' I stopped in my tracks; there was no answer from the men. 'My mum is just like Superman!' he exclaimed again. *I am?* I thought, slightly confused. I waited to listen where my son couldn't see me. 'She's adopted, just like Superman.'

'Oh,' I heard a man reply. When I entered the room, I almost felt embarrassed that he had revealed my adoption to these strangers. Yet I was flattered that my son connected me to his favourite superhero.

One night, a few days on, I had a powerful dream. I was offering to help a man find his birth daughter and my mum asked if I could help find a baby for her friends to adopt. I started screaming that I didn't believe in adoption, that a baby should stay with its mother and not be taken away. In a rage, I screamed over and over that adoption was wrong, and that if it really was necessary for the child to be taken away from its mother, the birth mother should be in touch regularly and be able to see her child. I gave birth the day after that dream.

The birth was much easier in many ways than my son's had been. Although the labour was intense, we played music and I sang at the top of my voice and danced my way around the room, much to the amusement of the nurses. Suddenly, at one point during transition and deep pain, I had this overwhelming certainty that the baby was a girl. As I sang along to the music, I felt such energy. It was so powerful. Her birth was so beautiful and she was so wanted! I felt sad for Pat and myself; no one should have to bring a baby into the world under those circumstances. How different it had been for us.

I pushed the baby out in fifteen minutes. 'It's a girl, it's a girl,' I said over and over. 'I have a boy and now I have a girl! How come I get to be so lucky?' The nurses and doctor laughed, and as a lullaby played in the background, I held my tiny, perfect daughter and felt instant love. How could I have doubted that I wouldn't have enough love for more than one child? As my doctor cleaned us up, she sang along to the lullaby too, and the atmosphere was tranquil and spiritual. It was a wonderful birth, just what I had hoped for. We named her Kayla Rae.

I truly enjoyed being a new mother again. It was not as intense as with Zach, but I had moments when I looked at Kayla and wondered how anyone could give up her baby. How could you do that, and if you do, how do you keep from going insane? Visions of her being stolen were just like the ones I had seen with Zach, but this time I refused to let them take control. I shouted, 'Go away! You are not going to spoil this time for me. We are safe. My baby is safe and I am allowed to be happy. I am allowed to have two children, just like other people.'

People say my daughter looks just like me, but I can't really believe that I was ever that pretty as a baby or as cute. Some days I look at her and wonder who her mother is. Then I realise it's me; I feel connected and I know she is part of me. Often I find myself scrutinising a huge photograph of my daughter. It is so familiar to me, yet it also feels odd. It takes me a moment to realise why: I am looking at someone who looks like me.

I love watching my children together; I can see their connection. I love the way Kayla smiles at Zach and I'm fascinated by their similarity. So this is what it's like to look like your sibling! I wonder whether I will always feel that way, if, for me, it will always feel strange to be in a blood-related family.

21
Birthday blues

My birthday is so horrendous, but for my daughter I have to make it perfect – a huge celebration. Delle

I never knew children like to talk about their birth until I had my own; it was something alien to me, a subject I didn't know how to approach. My children love to talk about how they came into the world, what they looked like, where they were before they were with me. It helped me understand that the reason my birth wasn't discussed was because it was too awkward for my parents to talk about. How do you explain to an adopted child that your mother gave you away? And yet the silence surrounding it made me want to know more.

My adoptive parents certainly celebrated my arrival at their home, but I was two months old. I had already had two mothers – my birth mother and a foster mother – and now my adoptive mother. I truly believe that even if a child is adopted on the day of its birth, the sense of abandonment will be the same and the grief will go unresolved. In recent years, some close friends of mine have suffered the deaths of people they love and I have watched them struggle with their grief. The anniversary of a death is a particularly difficult time. For adopted people, birthdays are an anniversary too, the anniversary of their separation and abandonment, the day their mothers gave them away. However, this phenomenon goes unacknowledged in our society.

The two weeks or so before and after my birthday have always been hard for me. A baby picks up on its mother's anxiety and disconnection *in utero*. The baby knows that it is going to be given away and experiences panic and fear for its survival because it knows it needs its mother to keep it alive. On the day of birth, a baby may or may not see its mother. One thing both mother and baby know is that they will be separated.

I have known adopted people who have such severe depression around their birthdays that they are literally incapable of doing anything constructive. I have seen them walk into adoption support meetings and share what they are feeling and for others to express that they too have the same experience. Their relief and surprise are genuine. It's comforting to know that I am not alone, that other adopted people have this experience too.

As I approach my birthday, I am able to observe myself a little more. I am able to catch myself in the process that I go through. It is very important that my birthday be acknowledged, yet I also want the day to be over. Even though I have been in reunion a long time, there is still a physical reaction of despair and sadness that surprises me. I find myself, without wanting to, feeling what I can now put into words: the separation from my mother. And these days, I think of my birth father too.

Not long ago, an adopted woman told me it was her daughter's first birthday. A lot of feelings were coming up for her – despair and panic at how she would get through the day emotionally. It reminded me of Zach's first birthday and how I felt. I didn't realise what was going on.

All I knew was I had to keep busy so I wouldn't feel. *Feel what?* Like I did at my own day of birth? Yet this day was different, it was a celebration of my child. How I wanted it to be perfect! Yes, I went over the top. I bought too many gifts, asked too many people, but I wanted everyone to know what a special day it was and for Zach to be the centre of attention. I wanted him to know that we remembered his birthday, that it was special. When it came time to cut the cake, I was a mess. How would I contain myself? When everyone sang to him, I barely managed, but I still wonder at the magnitude of those emotions. Why did I want to curl up and howl?

As a child, I knew that I was supposed to enjoy and be happy on my birthday, so I never let on the depression I felt. I didn't understand what was wrong with me. I remember one birthday when all the children were having a great time watching fireworks out of the long window overlooking our garden. Everyone made the right sounds of appreciation as the fireworks fizzed and popped, lighting up the night sky, but I felt such despair that I crept off to be alone. After a time I was able to join the party again. I was seven years old.

My birthday was always the time when I wondered about my birth mother. As a small child, I would look up at the big sky and wonder if she were standing under it too. Did she think of me on this day? Sometimes I could almost feel her, yet I worried that I had been forgotten. I carried that fear throughout life: Have I been forgotten? Do people remember me when I am not in sight? As a child, what was particularly hard was my inability to express myself. My mother had no inkling of what was going on inside me; I always hoped she would somehow be able to guess.

My first birthday celebration with my birth family was scary. I didn't want to go, but it seemed very important to Pat. I brought my girlfriend Virginia along to the restaurant for support. I was bombarded with presents. I think that

Pat wanted to make up for all those years she hadn't been able to give me something, and it was bittersweet. Guilt began to come back big and strong. How could I accept these presents? Did I have a right to them? How would my adoptive family feel if they knew what I was doing? I could feel Pat's emotion. There was so much to say, yet nobody did. Instead, we carried on in our awkwardness to do what one was supposed to do on birthdays. All those years apart and here we were together, celebrating. It felt so strange.

22
Telling the truth

I feel that not telling my daughters I am adopted is the same as not telling an adoptee they are adopted; it is who they are, it is their heritage. Hazel

I wondered how I would explain being adopted to Zach, who at the time was just under three-and-a-half years old. I still had the tendency to protect both families, but I knew I didn't want to lie to him or keep secrets. Yet at times it was easier to just not mention certain things, to not include certain people, especially when I still had my own issues to work through.

I was with Zach one day as he sat on the toilet and we were talking about our visit to London earlier that year, specifically the visit to Pat. I said, 'You know, Zach, she is your grandma too, like Grandma Jane,' (my mother). He listened as I told him I had been given to Grandma Jane because Grandma Pat couldn't take care of me. Zach wanted to know why Grandma Pat couldn't take care of me. I didn't know what to say, so I told him that it was because she was young and it was too hard for her. All the reasons I gave sounded strange even to me, not good enough reasons to be given way.

My son thought for a while and then asked, 'Was there a cord?' I hesitated, unsure of what he meant.

He asked again, 'Was there a cord?'

I finally understood. 'Between Grandma Jane and me?'

'Yes,' he said.

I shook my head. 'No, there wasn't.'

With that, he hopped off the toilet and went on to something else. I stood rooted to the floor for a moment. At only three-and-a-half, Zach really had got it!

When Kayla was fifteen months old, I became pregnant and again went into a strange state of denial. Jonathan kept asking me, 'Have you had your monthly yet?' I told him no and that it was fine. A couple of weeks later, he told me to get the test done and I moaned and groaned about how expensive pregnancy tests were and it was a waste of money. I kept up the complaining all the way into the bathroom as I took the test, then went dead silent.

'Told you,' he yelled from the other room.

I was scared to have another daughter. I couldn't explain to myself exactly why and decided I was definitely carrying a boy. Nevertheless, a week before I gave birth, I dreamed the baby was a girl. Unlike with my first two, I was able to deliver the new baby, Arden, without any artificial inducement to get the contractions moving. For some reason, this was really important to me. My friends couldn't understand why I decided to go for a natural birth. I didn't know either. It was just something I felt I had to do.

As I put our new daughter to my breast and enjoyed those sacred first few hours, I was certain that we were meant to be together and that Kayla and she would be true sisters. It meant they would have something I didn't have; it dawned on me that I'd been afraid of that too. I had a sister, yet we hadn't grown up together. Like my birth mother, I had a son and two daughters, except that I got to keep my two girls and Pat didn't.

As I watched Arden grow, I found myself searching my little daughter's face. She has her own look, yet there's a difference between her and my other children. Does she resemble my birth father? I look for clues in her face, her hair and her body. It's my only way of imagining what he may look like.

A few years ago, Zach overheard Jonathan and I talking about my birth father. He began to question me:

'What is a birth father? Why didn't you find him?'

I replied that I had tried, but that it was too hard with so little information.

Zach persisted. 'Why don't you try again?'

I sighed. 'I don't really know what else to do and it takes a lot of energy that I don't have right now.'

'What's his name?' my son asked.

'Vittorio. That's all I know.' I began to feel very strange discussing this with my son. Zach kept his steady eye on me and I looked away. I could feel the tears wanting to escape.

'Mummy,' he said solemnly, 'when I'm older, I'm going to help you find him.'

The tears came and I hugged him tightly. 'That's an incredibly kind thing for you to do for me.'

I still love babies and some days I'm really tempted to have more. I'm not one of those women who say they never want to be pregnant again. Recently I had a flash of understanding about why I feel this way. When I had my baby it was the first time I had ever experienced such a strong connection – physical, spiritual and emotional. Maybe it's the same for all mothers, I don't know. I remember thinking, *So this is what it's really like to feel a bond between mother and child.* There were no barriers. Even though I have a wonderful time with my children as they're growing up, I want to re-experience that feeling of total connection over and over again.

My feelings surrounding my adoption do not dominate

my life in the way that they used to. Having children has brought back long-dormant childhood memories. For instance, I had an extreme fear that my parents would die and that I would end up in a children's home. I would lie in bed at night and beg God not to take them from me. I also had nightmares about them dying and would sometimes go to their bedroom in the middle of the night to reassure myself that they were still breathing. I resumed these night checks with my own babies and continue them even now.

I continue to suffer separation anxiety from time to time. Perhaps it's just part of what it is to be a mother. Even when Arden was a baby I couldn't let even my husband take her for a walk without feeling uncomfortable, so I tell him. Irrational fears overwhelm me on some days but I won't let them take over my life. On the other hand, it was easier to parent Arden. I was able to do simple things that I was unable to do with Zach because of my terror of separation and my inability to distinguish him as a person apart from myself and my childhood feelings. For example, I can leave Arden in the bedroom with the door closed while she sleeps. I was unable to do that with Zach. I am able to go out more and leave the children with babysitters and enjoy my time away without calling every five minutes to make sure they are not only OK but still there.

Another way in which separation anxiety manifested itself was in the weaning of my three babies. The benefits of breastfeeding are inarguable, so I breastfed each one for more than a year. When it was time to wean Zach, I was shocked at the deep feelings of panic that came up for me. After talking with other adoptee mothers, though, it became clear that the fear of weaning was the fear of loss of connection, and loss of connection is like a death. Weaning the two younger children hasn't been much easier, but at least I have clarity about the feelings.

When Arden was a baby, I had another revelation. I lay

her down in bed, unable from sheer exhaustion to carry her any longer. She cried angrily that I had put her down, but as I watched her fight off the sleep she so desperately needed, I realised that letting her cry for a few moments didn't make me a bad mother. I was just a very tired mother, a mother still projecting my fears, my feelings of abandonment onto my baby. I sat next to her and whispered reassuring words and told her that I just couldn't keep carrying and rocking her, that I needed her to sleep. She fussed for a few moments, looked at me and fell asleep.

My children are not me. My work as a mother is to respect them and allow them to be whoever they are, guide them, teach them, love them fully without holding back, kiss them as much as they will let me, hold them tight and then let them go. Day to day, I focus as much as I can on being in the present moment with my children. I try to remember, when I am not too exhausted and burned out, that life is fleeting, that soon they will grow and leave the nest. Some days this is not easy, especially when fear leads the way. Today I feel wholeness, a sense of belonging, that I have never known before. I look into my children's eyes and they are familiar to me. It feels incredible. I love having a family.

As my children grow older, I find myself faced with a new challenge: honesty. I see already that I don't always want to include Pat as Grandma Pat in conversation with them for fear that they will say something to my parents. I know my mum and dad would find it hard if they knew the children called Pat their grandmother too. So here I am, repeating some of my old behaviour, living in the silence I grew up with.

I realise yet again that I have to stop protecting everyone else's feelings, that they have a right to feel whatever they feel, and that it is my children's birthright (like it is mine) to know their genetic heritage. Some days I am angry when

Pat sends a card to one of the children and signs it 'Grandma'. I think, *What right does she have to that title? She lost that privilege!* But at the same time, I want my children to feel free to ask questions about adoption, about both their families, without my unresolved baggage clouding their lives. They have a right to relationships with all members of my birth family and my adoptive family as well. I strive to make a home where it is safe for them to speak out and to have relationships without my feeling threatened. I know that the only way to accomplish this is to continually work on my issues and my prejudices, and not to use my children as pawns in any way.

As my children grow older, adoption is not anything strange to them; the fact that they have two grandmothers from my side is not complicated for them, they just enjoy having people around that give them love and presents. What is a little strange and something Zach, now eleven, is figuring out, is that my two mothers haven't met yet – he doesn't understand why as he seems so clearly to see how we are all connected to each other. It is, though, still difficult for any of my children to know why Pat couldn't raise me. When I tell them she was young and describe about society back then, it doesn't make sense to my children but they were all extremely shocked that you could get pregnant without being married!

Much to my husband's horror, I already find myself talking to my children about having babies and telling my husband that, if one of our girls came home pregnant young, there is no way that baby is going anywhere. He looks at me as if I'm mad. 'Yes, Zara. I totally know that and wouldn't want it any other way but really, why are you thinking abut this now? She is only five years old!'

As Zach has recently begun to learn about sex, I started worrying. 'What if he gets a girl pregnant and her mother makes her give up the baby and that's our first grandchild and I have no say in the matter . . .'

Jonathan looked at me. 'Oh my God, is this the stuff that you think about, that occupies your brain? He is eleven years old!'

I replied, 'Well, these things happen. We have to make sure they know!'

Arden, my five-year-old, has just understood about adoption and while we were in England last summer we were in the toilet (a place it seems my children like to have deep discussions) and she looked at me directly and said in a sing-song voice, 'Mum, you're adopted, aren't yooooou? I know you are.'

I said, 'Yes, do you know what it means?'

'Hmmm,' she thought, 'She didn't want you?'

One evening, after talking to Arden I asked Kayla to describe adoption, as I really wanted to know whether she understood or if it was just a word to her. This is what she said:

'You were in Pat's tummy and you grew. Grandma Jane came and someone cut a hole in Grandma Pat's tummy and then cut a hole in Grandma Jane's tummy. They very very carefully took you out of Grandma Pat's tummy,' Kayla did the hand movements as if she were carrying a baby, 'and placed you gently in Grandma Jane's tummy so that you could finish growing and be born safely.'

I was astounded and didn't quite know what to say at first. I didn't want her to feel embarrassed, so I carefully told Kayla, 'Actually you can't remove a baby from its mother's tummy and then place it in another mummy. The baby needs to grow in one place, otherwise it wouldn't survive.'

Kayla started laughing and giggling. 'Oh, silly me,' she said 'of course you can't. It's just that's what I had always thought. I always thought that was what happened to you.'

What I understood so clearly was that if my daughter, who wasn't adopted, had pictured adoption to be like that, then no wonder I and so many other adopted children had let our imaginations take over. If an adult doesn't explain things to a child, then the child is just left with her or his own mind. Their story could be anything and it won't necessarily be positive. Often children think the worst, a common conclusion being 'I was adopted because there is something wrong with me.'

Kayla is the daughter who resembles me the most. Sometimes I literally do a doubletake when she walks past me. It took me a while to realise what it felt like to have a small person around that looked so much like me. 'I feel like I have been replaced,' I finally admitted, 'That somehow I don't exist any more.'

We took all the children swimming and I watched as they all got in and out of the pool, their bodies all tanning the same colour, their hair bleached by the sun, and I was fascinated. I started getting excited, 'Look, look!' Jonathan glanced over quickly, wondering for a second what was wrong. 'Jonathan isn't it amazing? Look at them! They all look so much alike. They look the same. Isn't it so weird?'

He peered at me, squinting in the sun. 'Zara, it's not weird; they are related. This is what it is like to be in a family where we look alike. It isn't weird at all, it's normal.'

23
Letting go

When I nursed and cared for my babies, especially my firstborn, I felt that I was in some way nurturing my own baby self, the one whom no one had welcomed to the world with love. Octavia

In the early years of my recovery, while attending meetings, my skin crawled as I heard people talk about their "inner child". I thought they were pathetic, that they used the idea as an excuse to act childishly and not take responsibility for the fact that they were now grown-ups. My friends and I would laugh at their expense. Yet why, when I sat in those meetings and heard the sharing, was I not only embarrassed at their honesty but also uncomfortable and deeply sad? I had spent most of my life to that point unwilling and unable to show anybody my pain. I was never able to sit still for a moment – I rushed about smoking cigarettes, taking drugs and talking on the phone. When I felt that familiar pang deep in my stomach, I knew what to do: call a friend, anything but wait to see what came up.

In that early period, I was cynical about everyone. I still

couldn't show much vulnerability, and there were many ways to stop feeling other than taking drugs: compulsive talking, reading *Hello* magazine, obsessing about someone else's life, or just busying myself with tasks. Sitting still can be a struggle even today, yet when I allow myself the time to sit quietly, it is always beneficial. Sadness passes a lot quicker if I simply allow myself to cry. The most liberating part is the softness of heart that comes with it, the insight and ability to see others' pain and joy, to break out of my isolation and rejoin the human race. Until I had experienced my grief, I was incapable of feeling joy. The two are intertwined.

Today I am happy to say that I experience much joy in my life. When I don't, it is because I am afraid to allow it in for fear of loss. To fully love another human being is indeed fraught with risk, yet if I had chosen not to face myself, I would have missed out on the greatest gift in life.

When a person goes through a severe trauma – the sudden death of a loved one, rape, an automobile accident – their world is rocked to the very core. They can feel as if they have lost their foundation, and their trust in life may disappear as they try to find new meaning. The good news is that friends, family and professional counsellors can recognise the trauma and acknowledge their pain.

For those of us who are adopted, there is no life before the trauma. Often it takes place *in utero*, so there is no memory of feeling whole and secure. When the adopted baby is brought home by her new parents there is, of course, much celebration. But while Mum and Dad are showing off their new baby to relatives and friends, laughing and talking with all the joy they feel, the baby is quietly wondering, 'Who are these people? This woman doesn't smell like my mother. Where did my mummy go?' The baby grows up with her loss unacknowledged and unresolved. Yet at some point, the body can no longer contain the emotions. They have to be expressed and will find a way to come out, often in destructive ways.

What astounds me now is that, even with all the knowledge I have acquired, the work I have done and the many people within the adoption community whom I have met along the way and who I know have had experiences similar to mine, I still have days when I want to isolate myself or when I feel totally detached from the rest of the world. It's like a physical reaction that seems to happen within myself and sometimes, when I am locked in that place, I still don't know how to get out and reconnect within my marriage. This can be really difficult. Commitment can still be an issue; I always seem to have one foot out of the door.

When I was pregnant with my second child, I said to my husband, 'You know, this really is a big commitment now.'

'What?' answered Jonathan, looking confused.

'This pregnancy; us having another child.'

'Zara, we have one child and we are married. Isn't that commitment already?'

When I recounted the conversation to Marlou Russell, she commented, 'Yes, so much easier to leave with one child than two, isn't it?' I laughed.

I look back at the years of drug-taking, shouting at my mother, running off and partying, the thoughts of separating myself from my husband and my children when it gets too hard, and see that all these thoughts and actions were to protect myself from the grief of loss that can feel as if it will kill me. I carry it even today; it still comes up when I least expect it, just when I think I've finally been able to let go.

When we lived in LA (not really through any great calling, but basically because in LA most of the pre-schools are attached to religious institutions), we started attending synagogue. Even though I have not participated in my faith in recent years, I felt more comfortable sending Zach to a school whose sponsor was at least familiar to me.

Recently, during a group discussion, our rabbi asked us to think about how we felt about being Jews. He asked us to reach back into childhood for memories of faith and tradition, so that we could bring them to consciousness when we needed them. He told the story of an old woman who lived in a convalescent home. Every Friday night, she imagined herself lighting the Shabbat candles and saying the prayers, even though she was just sitting in her chair. It brought her great comfort.

As the rabbi continued, I began to feel very uncomfortable. I had flashes of our family sitting around the table at Passover, reading prayers and eating. I remembered going to synagogue as a child and I saw the faces of people I hadn't thought about in many years. But what was most distinct was that, even though I remembered moments of enjoying the familiarity of the Jewish traditions, it was one of the places where I felt most like an outsider. As a teenager, I watched the other Jewish girls and yet I didn't feel like them. I felt different in many ways, not just physically. Sometimes they would say, 'You don't look Jewish.'

The others in the group asked me to share. I found myself saying for the first time that I had never felt Jewish. I had never been able to embrace Judaism because, as an adoptee, I was never sure if that's really who I was. Mum had always assured me that my birth mother had been Jewish, but for some reason I never believed her. So even though I wanted so badly to feel a part of Judaism, I felt only emptiness, misplacement. I cannot emphasise too much what a revelation this was for me. Up until that point, I had never understood that my adoption had kept me apart from not only my family but from God as well. It shows me again how important it is to tell an adopted child who they are on all sides, so they can truly embrace each part of themselves.

Even though it has felt extremely liberating for me to

finally make that connection, the truth is I am half-Italian. There is a whole side to me that I don't know anything about. It is not enough to say I am a Jew because my mother is Jewish; it does not fulfill that yearning to know my Italian side. Today, I find myself watching my children with their father and thinking how they all fit together. It is still hard some days to feel that I, too, am part of this unit. Most people, whether they get along with their families or not, don't even need to think about a sense of connection. They share the same bloodline, the same heritage; it is a spiritual connection. It's just there. I am not saying there is no spiritual connection with my adoptive family, only that as a child I didn't feel it. Paradoxically, since I have been reunited with my birth family – and especially since I've become a mother – I feel more connected to my adoptive family and feel more a part of them.

Being a parent is the hardest work I love to do. From everything I have read and from all the mothers I've spoken to, I realise more and more that it is up to me to not pass down my baggage to my children. Since I have carried both my adoptive and my birth mothers' feelings and fears, I am still challenged when it comes to separating out what truly belongs to me. The commitment to bringing emotionally healthy children into adulthood forces me to continue to work through my difficulties and take responsibility for my stuff.

I have seen already how my insecurity can affect my children: there are days when I'm not sure they love me and when I am scared that my daughters and I will go through the same painful clashes that my mother and I endured. Sometimes I catch myself projecting my unresolved conflicts onto my daughter. I have to keep being reminded – or reminding myself – that she is not me; she has her own feelings about life. I hope that she will see situations in a very different way to me. The main fact is that she is not adopted, so that makes us different from the start. She won't have to spend her childhood looking for her mother on every street and I will not have to constantly be on the lookout for my child, nor deal with the pain of infertility.

There are days when I am exhausted and need some time alone, and the last thing I want to do is be patient, tolerant and loving. Sometimes I tell my children, 'I am sorry, but I am not having a good day. It's not your fault.' And they tell me honestly, 'Yes Mum, you are being mean today' or 'You're a grump' or, as Zach called me after attending Jewish pre-school, 'You're a mean old Pharoah.'

I love having children and doing all the mummy things. When Zach was three years old, he sang with his preschool and I sat proudly at the front, tears streaming down my face. He looked on, horrified, from the stage. The next time he performed he said, 'Mum, you can only sit in the front row if you don't cry.' I assured him that I wouldn't, that I just got so emotional and felt so proud seeing him up there. Nevertheless, the night came and he stood at the front of the stage and yelled out to me for all to hear, 'Mum, don't cry, OK?'

'OK,' I promised. I just about managed to hold myself together. Now that my children are getting older I have to be even more careful about embarrassing them in front of their friends.

Zach wants to do sleepovers and recently he was invited to sleep on a submarine for a Boy Scouts' trip. I found myself asking him, 'Do you really want to go?'

'Yes Mum. Duh! Are you kidding? It's a submarine.'

I asked him again later. 'Zach, do you really want to go? Are you ready to go?' Then I laughed and said, 'Oh, it's me who isn't ready.'

He raised his eyes, 'Mum!'

Zach has been to a few sleepovers and I don't really like it. I can't wait for him to come home. I worry that he'll lie awake all night, as I did all those years ago with my friend and her family in Spain, unable to sleep when of course it's *my* anxiety.

Last year my children really wanted a guinea pig from the kindergarten teacher – babies had just been born and were ready to be taken home. I watched the teacher as she brought down the cage containing three guinea pigs – mum, dad and baby – but before she handed over the baby, Fluffy, I asked her if I could have a few moments alone with Fluffy's mother. She looked at me a little strangely. I knelt down by the cage and told the mother that I would take good care of her baby and whispered all kinds of reassuring things into the guinea pig's ear. The teacher eyed me all the time, probably remembering a conversation I had had with her some time ago about adoption, and said firmly, 'Zara, if Fluffy stays with his mother he will have sex with her. It is really time for him to leave.'

24
Full circle

My birth mother is willing to go only so far in her own healing. She is not willing to go back to when she had me, which puts a roadblock in our relationship. I seem to trigger her seventeen-year-old that gave birth to me, and she is full of shame when she goes back there. It's just explosive – it's the same explosive energy I had to work through in my therapy. But she doesn't have anyone to talk to. Iris

It has certainly been a long haul to get to where I am today in regard to my relationships with both my families. At the beginning of our reunion Pat and I struggled greatly. She was angry at me for being the way I was. She did not understand why I needed to know who my birth father was and told me that I would never find him. She wrote me letters that were hurtful and full of anger. I wrote back as best I could, trying not to dump on her all the rage I felt. I attempted to detach and understand that it wasn't about me, that I had become the target for all the pain and anger that she felt towards her own family for the way they had handled her pregnancy.

It was a very challenging time for me and, for a while, I

broke off all communication. I told Pat that I had to stop opening her letters, they hurt too much, and I felt she needed help. I knew I had to concentrate on my own recovery and, even then, many years passed by before I got the help I needed from adoption professionals. What Pat and I both needed was someone to explain that we were triggering each other's initial loss and that we couldn't fix each other. We each had to deal with our losses separately.

My brother always told me he had no interest in finding a mother who didn't want him, but at the age of thirty-six, he changed his mind. While he was in the process of searching, he began to call me on the phone for long talks. I felt honoured that Graham would confide in me. I was also interested in all the information he acquired. I felt as if I was in it with him and knew what he was going through. During those conversations, we began to talk in a way that we had never done before. I was able to share with him my feelings of growing up adopted and it helped us heal our relationship. We both gained a much deeper understanding of each other.

Sadly, Graham's mother has not been ready to meet him (so far) and I imagine that is a terrible rejection for him. Nevertheless, his sister and he have developed a close, warm relationship. I was lucky enough to meet her on a visit to London in the summer of 1999. I felt quite nervous and have to admit that, even though I was happy to hear about his reunion, I felt a slight pang of jealousy that they were such good friends. I wondered how I would fit into his life now that he had his birth sister. I also felt a little annoyed that she hadn't had to go through all the years of his childhood and his drug days, and could enjoy him now as a grown man.

I opened the door to a woman who was undoubtedly my brother's blood sister. I was fascinated. They had the same smile, they looked alike. Well, of course they would look alike, wouldn't they? They are full-blood siblings. But, to me, it was a surreal moment and one that I will always remember as the three of us – Graham and his two sisters – standing together. We sisters, both so much a part of him and his life, were strangers to one another. I sat them next to each other on the sofa and took photos. The whole time I was thinking, 'They fit! They look alike!'

Graham and I talk from time to time and usually see one another when I come to London. Recently, we've had more contact owing to our parents' situation, especially my mother's health. It's not easy for either of us and some days I can feel the tension. Nevertheless, we've been able to speak about how we felt as children in terms of the family dynamic and both find it comforting to know that we share similar feelings.   It's just sad that we didn't know how to talk about it years ago. Our relationship has changed: I'm no longer obsessed with how he is doing and watching his every move. I respect his decisions in life and wish him well and want the best for him. I haven't seen Graham's sister again, but I know he still shares a close relationship with her and I'm happy for him that he has that peace.

I wish I could tell you that reuniting with my birth family fixed everything in my life. It didn't. What it did do was to fill a lot of empty spaces in my heart. Just by knowing the facts, the real truth, I have been forced to give up the fantasy and look at it all squarely in the eye. This has brought up tremendous pain, deep feelings of abandonment and despair that I know now were always there, buried deep in my heart. Reunion began the process of feeling all these emotions. It was like slogging through a swamp full of alligators and snakes and unseen predators. I am not sorry I found my birth family. It was something I needed to do for myself. I am sorry, though, that it was not all that I had hoped for. Only later did I realise that my expectations had not been realistic.

In situations where the mother really doesn't want contact or the child has been abandoned, it is equally important to acknowledge the loss and to respect the child's heritage and, if possible, have some relations with other blood relatives. Recently I was talking with some people about adoption. We had a heated debate. They said, 'But adoption is good for the child. Where would some children be without it? Your adoptive parents are your parents, aren't they? Does it matter about where you came from?' My reply was, and will always be, the same. 'Yes, they are my parents, but unlike those who haven't been adopted, I also have another set of parents. I know my adoptive parents love me and I love them, but I have a different connection with them than I would experience if I had been raised in my birth home. I still need to know who my birth parents are.'

I am sorry that my adoptive parents were not given the information when they adopted me that is potentially available today. Maybe it would have made being parents easier for them and less painful when they learned of my brother's and my addictions; perhaps it would have eliminated some of the grief we put them through. I am sorry too that it has taken my mother and I, especially, so long to work through these issues and to respect one another for who we are. I realise that the grief I felt most of my life surrounding my lack of knowledge of my birth mother wasn't just about that. I also experienced tremendous grief over the fact that my adoptive mother and I never really got along, and I am sure she has too. It is incredibly sad when two people who genuinely love each other misconnect at every turn, without understanding why.

As I was doing further research for this book, my birth mother asked to contact my adoptive mother. I was wary to ask her as, for the last couple of years, my adoptive mother has been very ill, but I did pass on the message. My adoptive mother was not at all sure that, after all these years, it was worth them talking and I could tell that she felt threatened. After all this time of me being in reunion, it was still hard for her, which made me feel terribly sad. I reassured her, suggesting she think about it and do what she felt comfortable with.

That night, I dreamed that my two mothers met: my adoptive mother was stoic in the dream and my birth mother cried. I spent the whole time trying to find my wallet; I had lost all my credit cards and my driving licence. I couldn't find them anywhere. I was frantic. When I woke up the meaning was so clear: my identity had been lost.

Both my mothers have told me that they had always wanted to have contact but whenever I asked them, years ago, they declined. Maybe I never pushed it back then because I was scared of how they would respond. I don't know why, after eighteen years, they decided to reach out, but they did. Recently, they talked for a brief while on the phone and it was OK for both of them – they called within minutes of each other to tell me. I felt quite relieved and happy for them. No decisions were made about meeting but my adoptive mother said she would call Pat some time. My two worlds were finally coming together and it felt good.

Since becoming a mother, I have been much more able to put myself in both my birth mother's and adoptive mother's situations. I have felt compassion for both. As for my adoptive mother, if I could not have had my own children, I do not know how I would have managed. I have truly seen the loss that infertility can bring to a woman. Having children has meant everything to me; I feel extremely sad that my mother didn't have this experience and yet proud of her for the brave way she has tried to overcome her feelings. Coming from her generation, I know this hasn't been easy.

As for my birth mother, she was only a baby herself. She had neither job skills nor resources nor real support. Even so, the baby in me will never understand why she didn't fight to keep me. Therefore, I am grateful for the stories that other birth mothers have told me. They have helped me to understand that they are not merely women who just didn't care, or that giving up their babies meant nothing to them.

I have also learned more about Pat's family and her parents' unwillingness to help her during her pregnancy. Appearing as a good, solid family was far more important than bringing shame and grief upon themselves. They were prisoners of a society not yet free of the straightjacket of the Fifties. No matter what other members of the family thought or tried to offer, for my parents keeping me was never considered an option. Do I understand and forgive them for their attitude? For deciding that appearing respectable to the outside world was more important than my welfare? I feel some compassion and forgiveness because I know that, ultimately, their decision didn't free anyone from the truth. They simply spent years trying to bury it all.

As for myself, the part of me that still believes that I was given up because there was something wrong with me will diminish with the passage of time. But I feel sad when I think about all those years of not really knowing the truth. Would it have made me feel better about myself if I had known my story? Or would it still have taken me this long to understand what it all meant?

Every time I learn more about my beginnings, I experience a new freedom. I spoke just recently with an aunt who told me she had knitted baby clothes for me. At my uncles' request, she had gone out and bought the best baby clothes she could find before taking me to my foster mother. This aunt had been there when I was handed over and it had affected her deeply.

Learning about these little details has made me feel good. As a child, I had never taken into consideration that others might have had feelings about me. How could I? No one had told me. I was just a child with a limited but vivid imagination.

Time is a healer but only with a great deal of patience and soul searching. I spent years blaming both my mothers for my problems, really believing that if they would just only understand me and see where I was coming from, everything would be all right, but that would never have been the solution. You cannot give something you haven't got – today I understand that phrase – and you cannot push someone further along their journey than they already are.

I have had to look deep within myself and, corny as it sounds, I have had to learn to forgive and gain compassion because it is too hard to live as an angry person when you don't take drugs! In spite of myself, my heart has softened in ways I didn't think would ever be possible. When I am compassionate to any human being and accept their failings, miracles really do happen. I think that I can finally say that I have many more moments of feeling that way towards both my mothers. I have tried to step into their shoes and realise that neither of their paths has been easy.

I strongly believe that to heal from the adoption wound we all have to grieve our losses individually and then together. I don't regret finding my birth family, however hard it was. It has given me a sense of self that I didn't have before. I regret that I didn't know how many years it would take to work through all the difficulties and that I didn't expose myself to the professional help that was available to me sooner. I am totally against closed records as is the practice in much of the US. It's not confusing to know who your birth mother is. *It's confusing to not know.* It's not surprising that adopted people are the largest minority of those who are institutionalised or who suffer from various forms of addiction or mental health problems.

To any adopted person searching for help and support, I say this: find people who *really* know and understand the adoption experience and stay away from people who *think* they know. Avoid like the plague those who are just interested in being a part of your reunion stories because it sounds like fun. Be open to professional counselling to understand and help process all the conflicting emotions you may feel so that your reunion can be the best possible experience; so that you, as an adoptee, can pass on to your children the joy in their arrival that you never felt was connected to your own.

I continue to go to my twelve-step support groups and abstain from drugs and alcohol; I take life a day at a time. I have learnt that, regardless of how many years it has been, I am still the same Zara who has moments of wanting to annihilate myself and I cannot ever afford to take risks again.

I share my experiences with other members of the adoption triad in the US and recently, after contacting London's Barnet Adoption Team, the local authority I was adopted through, I have been speaking with others touched by adoption in the UK. I feel like I have come full circle.

Epilogue

As 2007 draws to a close, my relationships with both my adoptive family and my birth family are changing. I have less anger, I have more understanding and the paradox is that finding my birth family has made me feel more a part of my adoptive family than ever before. I always want to tell adoptive parents, when they are scared, that this is a common experience: once the adopted child knows where she or he comes from they are able to appreciate their adoptive families so much more. They *are* my family and I truly love them. Our relationship today is better than it has ever been.

Pat recently called me about a television programme she had seen about daughters reuniting with their fathers. She told me she could hardly get her make-up on that morning because she was crying so much. She asked me whether she ought to write in to the programme to see if they could help me locate my birth father. I said, 'Yes!' Even though it's a long shot, anything is worth a try. This was the first time that Pat had ever offered to help me with my search. That willingness was what I had wanted so much in the beginning. But I have learned that healing takes time and that gives me hope that all our relationships can continue to grow.

The hardest times are when my expectations are too high, when I want so badly for both families to understand me. I have learned the painful lesson that I am the only one who can identify and heal my wounds. Neither of my families can do that for me; they too have wounds that I cannot heal.

I also have been shown in recent years how adoption affects the life cycle. My adoptive mother is still unwell, at one point close to dying, and is dependent on various medications to keep her alive. When it looked as if she was failing, I found myself re-experiencing panic attacks that I hadn't had in years – the same familiar feelings that I had as a child when I was so desperately worried something would happen to her.

I had to remind myself that I was a grown up now and that, if she did pass away, it didn't mean I would not be able to manage. I would be able to live without her. I was struck again by the intensity of my feelings. After all, I have explored this subject for years, yet here I was again, the body memory as clear as it was all those decades ago.

Over my years as a mother, I've continued to sing and write. While my babies had a bath, the children would play and I would sing away. As they get older they often come into my room and ask me to 'turn down my amp' and Arden, at two years old, told her preschool teacher that 'Mummy is doing a gig tonight'. As I drive off to play at some venue, a mother of three, I sometimes wonder myself what I am doing! The truth is that my music has saved me over and over again from myself. It is so much more of a gift than I ever understood.

In my twenties, I was so caught up in the need for success, for a sense of achievement to make me feel special and complete. I realise now that, when that was my focus, the music didn't have the same benefit; I didn't enjoy or write in the way I do when I am writing and singing purely for the love of it or simply from the need to express what is going on in my life. I am incredibly grateful for being able to sing and I really don't know how I would live without it. Some days Zach will come in the room and listen and say, 'Hey Mum, that's a good song.' It means such a lot to me.

When Zach received a certificate for student of the month for creativity, I was taken aback, not only by my motherly pride, but also by my reaction. My children love to make books on subjects that interest them, just as I did as a child. Why is it strange to me that my Kayla loves to draw and write stories and that both my girls love to sing and dance? They enjoy sports the way I did; Arden can run as fast as I could as a small child. I have enjoyed those things all my life.

My children have become my reflection. I can finally look at myself in the mirror and know that I am not some unique, one-of-a-kind alien that landed on Earth with no explanation. I belong. I am connected. I have a birth story too.

Resources

RECOMMENDED READING

This is a list of adoption-related books. If you are searching or reunited, please take the time to read as many as you can. They will help you understand birth mothers, adopted people and adoptive parents, as well as reunions and all the issues that go with adoption.

Brodzinsky D M, Schechter M D and Hening R M (1992) *Being Adopted: The lifelong search for self*, New York/London: Doubleday

Campbell N (2005) *Blue-eyed Boy*, Basingstoke/Oxford: Pan Books

Eldridge S (2005) *25 Things Adopted Kids Wish their Adoptive Parents Knew*, New York: Bantam Doubleday Dell Publishing Group Inc.

Elliott S (2005) *Love Child: A memoir of adoption and reunion, loss and love*, London: Vermilion

Feast J and Philpot T (2003) *Searching Questions: Identity, origins and adoption*, London: BAAF

Hamner K (2000) *Whose Child? An adoptee's healing journey from relinquishment through reunion and beyond*, Gainesville, FL: Triad Publishing

Howe D and Feast J (2003) *Adoption, Search and Reunion: The long-term experience of adopted adults*, London: BAAF

Jackson K and McKinley C (1996) 'Sisters: a reunion story', in Wadia-Ellis S (ed), *The Adoption Reader: Birth mothers, adoptive mothers and adopted daughters tell their stories*, London: The Women's Press

Kay J (1991) *The Adoption Papers*, Newcastle Upon Tyne: Bloodaxe Books

Lifton B J (1977, last reprint 2006) *Twice Born: Memoirs of an adopted daughter*, New York: St Martin's Press

Lifton B J (1988) *Lost and Found: The adoption experience*, New York: Harper Perennial

Lifton B J (1995) *Journey of the Adopted Self: A quest for wholeness*, New York: Basic Books

Mulholland J (2007) *Special & Odd*, London: BAAF

National Organisation for the Counselling of Adoptees and Parents (NORCAP) (2000) *Searching for Family Connections*, Wheatley, Oxon: NORCAP

Pool H (2005) *My Father's Daughter*, London: Penguin

Pannor R, Baran A and Sorosky (1989) *The Adoption*

Triangle, San Antonio, Texas: Corona Publishing

Rendall J (2006) *Garden Hopping: An adoption memoir*, Edinburgh: Canongate Books

Robinson E Burns (2000) *Adoption and Loss: The hidden grief*, Mitcham, South Australia: Jacobyte Books; www.cloverpublications.com

Russell M (1996) *Adoption Wisdom*, Los Angeles, CA: Broken Branch Productions

Schaefer C (1992) *The Other Mother: A true story*, New York: Soho Press

Soll J (2006) *Adoption Healing: A path to recovery*, Woodbury, NY: Juneau Press

Thomas V and Kelly J (1981, last reprint, 2004) *The Secret Life of the Unborn Child*, London: Time Warner Paperbacks

Trinder L, Feast J and Howe D (2004) *The Adoption Reunion Handbook*, Chichester: John Wiley & Sons

Triseliotis J, Feast J and Kyle F (2005) *The Adoption Triangle Revisited: A study of adoption, search and reunion experience*, London: BAAF

Verrier N (1993) *The Primal Wound*, Baltimore: Gateway Press

WEBSITES

These are some useful websites for the UK, followed by a few that I have found useful in the USA.

UK

Adoption About
www.adoption.about.com

Adoptiontracker.com
www.adoptiontracker.com

British Association for Adoption and Fostering (BAAF)
www.baaf.org.uk

Mothers Apart from Their Children
www.matchmothers.org

Natural Parents Network (NPN)
www.n-p-n.fsnet.co.uk

NCH Action for Children
www.nchafc.org.uk

UK Birth-Adoption Register.com
www.ukbirth-adoptionregister.com

USA

Adopting.org: especially for adoptees
www.adopting.org/adoptees.html

Adoption Excellence Institute
www.bestofbothworlds.org

American Adoption Congress
www.americanadoptioncongress.org

Concerned United Birthparents
www.cubirthparents.com

National Adoption Clearinghouse: Introduction to search
www.calib.co/naic/adoptees/search.htm

Reunite.com
www.reunite.com

ORGANISATIONS

The following national and regional organisations are based in the UK, Scotland and the Republic of Ireland. A list of US resources is available on my website: zarahphillips.com

England and Wales

Adoption Support
Suite A, 6th Floor, Albany House
Hurst Street
Birmingham B5 4BD
Tel: 0121 666 6014
www.adoptionsupport.co.uk

Adoption UK (providing support for adoptive families)
46 The Green
South Bar Street
Banbury OX16 9AB
Tel: 01295 752240
Helpline: 0870 7700 450
www.adoptionuk.com

After Adoption (Head Office)
1214 Chapel Street
Salford
Manchester M3 7NH
Helpline: 0161 839 4930
Email: information@afteradoption.org.uk

Barnardo's
Tanners Lane
Barkingside, Ilford
Essex 1G6 1QG
Tel: 0208 550 8822
www.barnardos.org.uk

Barnardo's Cymru
11–15 Columbus Walk
Brigantine Place, Atlantic Wharf
Cardiff CF10 4BZ
Tel: 0292 049 3387

Catholic Children's Society (Westminster)
(formerly the Catholic Crusade of Rescue Society)
73 St Charles Square
London W10 6EJ
Tel: 0208 969 5305
www.catholicchildrenssociety.org.uk

The Children's Society (formerly the Church of
England Waifs and Strays)
Post Adoption and Care: Counselling Research Project
91 Queen's Road
London SE15 2EZ
Tel: 0207 732 9089
www.childrenssociety.org.uk

National Organisation for the Counselling of Adoptees and their Parents (NORCAP)
112 Church Road
Wheatley
Oxfordshire OX33 1LU
Tel: 01865 875000
www.norcap.org.uk

Post-Adoption Centre
5 Torriano Mews
Torriano Avenue
London NW5 2RZ
Tel: 020 7284 0555
Tel: 0870 777 2197 (Advice line)
www.postadoptioncentre.org.uk

South West Adoption Network (SWAN)
Leinster House
Leinster Avenue, Knowle
Bristol BS4 1AL
Tel: 0845 601 2459 (Helpline)
www.swan-adoption.org.uk

Scotland

Barnardo's Scottish Adoption Advice Service
(West Scotland only)
16 Sandyford Place
Glasgow G3 7NB
Tel: 0141 339 0772 (Advice line)

Birth Link
Family Care
21 Castle Street
Edinburgh EH2 3DN
Tel: 0131 225 6441
www.birthlink.org.uk

Group for Adopted People (GAP) (Central Scotland)
Jan Morris (Co-ordinator)
Rock Community Project
The Rock Centre, 1st Floor
61–63 Murray Place
Stirling FK8 1AP
Tel: 0178 685 0733
Email: gapscotland@yahoo.co.uk

Post Adoption Central Support (PACS)
Rena Phillips (Co-ordinator)
Tel: 0125 978 1545
www.postadoptioncentralsupport.org

Scottish Adoption Association (East Scotland only)
2 Commercial Street
Edinburgh EH6 6JA
Tel: 0131 553 5060
www.scottishadoption.org

Northern Ireland

ADOPT – Northern Ireland
VSB, The Peskett Centre
2/2a Windsor Road
Belfast BT9 FFQ
Tel: 0289 038 2353

Church of England Adoption Society
Church of England House
61–67 Donegall Street
Belfast BT1 2QH
Tel: 0289 023 3885
www.cofiadopt.org.uk

Republic of Ireland

The Adoption Board
Shelbourne House
Shelbourne Road, Ballsbridge
Dublin 4
Tel: 00353 1 669 1392

Adopted People's Association
27 Templeview Green
Clare Hill
Dublin 13
Tel: 00353 1 867 4033
www.adoptionireland.com

Barnardo's Adoption Advice Service
Chirstchurch Square
Dublin 8
Tel: 00353 1 453 0355
Tel: 0141 339 0772 (Advice line)

BIRTH CERTIFICATES

For birth certificates apply to:

Public Search Room
St Catherine's House
10 Kingsway
London WC2B 6JB

The Registrar General
Adopted Children's Register
Titchfield, Fareham
Hants PO 15 5RV
(for England and Wales)
www.gro.gov.uk/gro/content/

General Registrar offices

Registrar General (England and Wales)
The General Register Office
Adoption Section
Smedley Hydro, Trafalgar Road
Birkdale, Southport PR8 2HH
Tel: 0151 471 4313
www.gro.gov.uk/gro/content/adoptions/
In England and Wales, adopted people aged 18 and over are entitled to a copy of their original birth certificate. The Registrar General operates the government Adoption Contact Register for adoptees aged 18 and over and birth relatives.

The General Register Office (Scotland)
New Register House
3 West Register Street
Edinburgh EH1 3YT
Tel: 0131 334 0380
www.gro-scotland.gov.uk
In Scotland, adopted people aged 16 and over are entitled to a copy of their original birth certificate.

The Registrar General (Northern Ireland)
Oxford House
49–55 Chichester Street
Belfast BT1 4HL
Tel: 0289 025 2000
www.groni.gov.uk
In Northern Ireland, adopted people aged 18 and over are entitled to a copy of their original birth certificate.

The Registrar General
Joyce House
8–11 Lombard Street East
Dublin 2
Tel: 35 31 6711 863

Records of births, marriages and deaths: England and Wales

Family Records Centre
1 Myddleton Street
London EC1R 1UW
Tel: 0845 603 7788
Certificate enquiries: certificate.services@ons.gov.uk
www.familyrecords.gov.uk/frc